The Left Has Always Been Right

A Reality-based History of American Politics

R P Ericksen

Copyright © 2012 R P Ericksen

All rights reserved.

ISBN: 1-4775-3924-7
ISBN-13: 9781477539248

TABLE OF CONTENTS

Preface	vii
Self-evident Truths: An Introduction	1
Chapter 1: Democracy	13
Chapter 2: Gender	39
Chapter 3: Race	65
Chapter 4: Money	91
Chapter 5: War	127
Fixing our Mistakes: A Conclusion	163
Epilogue: Same-Sex Marriage	173

PREFACE

This book is based on a simple claim rooted in a measured look at more than two centuries of American history: The left has always been right. I am not discussing bell-bottom trousers or tie-dyed shirts. I am not even discussing rock and roll. But I am talking about big issues, the most important issues we have faced as a nation. I am talking about democracy, about gender, about race, about economics, and about war. The left has always been right about these things. As we look back on our history, it seems absolutely clear that conservatives have been wrong on democracy, gender and race. I will argue that they also have been and remain on the wrong side of our nation's relationship to money and to war.

Conservatives by definition believe in conserving the past. They want to preserve longstanding tradition. If we acknowledge—as we must—that various forms of injustice existed in our past, we also have to acknowledge that conservatives at the time wanted to preserve the injustice. It was in their nature. Conservatives in their day spoke out against democracy. They wanted to limit the vote to white men who owned property, claiming that only those men could be trusted to guide our national course. Conservatives in their day argued against women's equality, claiming that God created women to serve in the household, to be obedient, and to acknowledge their subservient position in relation to men. Conservatives argued the same thing about God's plan for African Americans, both during and after the era of slavery—an expectation of service, obedience, and subservience. We do not accept any of these positions today. Why? Because progressives eventually prevailed. It was advocates on the left who convinced us of the injustice of these longstanding traditions and the need for change.

Everyone now accepts that these progressive changes were appropriate and necessary. No respectable conservative today would argue for turning back the clock on democracy, gender, or race. Conservatives who do advocate turning back the clock are relegated to the whacky rightwing fringe of American politics and not taken seriously. They are in the Ku Klux Klan or the White Aryan Supremacy movement. The rest of us agree that an equal right to vote, equal rights for women, and equal rights for black Americans are appropriate. But what does that tell us about the conservatives who fought those changes? What does it tell us about residual ideas that some conservatives might still be hiding today? Even without that possibility of hidden racism or sexism on the right, what does it tell us about *conservatism*?

On the issue of money, today's Republican Party is adamantly against raising taxes on the richest 1% of Americans, even though a majority of the public advocates that as one important element in any solution to our present economic frustrations. Even a majority of Republican voters agrees, differing with Republicans in Congress. Conservatives also argue for free-market capitalism and deregulation. Do they want clean water, clean air, or basic safety in the workplace? All of these things come from government intervention, not from the free market. Do they want protection from Ponzi schemes or insider trading? Once again, only government action has protected us. Do they want to avoid another Great Depression? Before Franklin Roosevelt in the 1930s, we had a depression every decade or so. In the eighty years since Roosevelt invented activist government, we have never had another!

In terms of war, conservatives tell us to be tough. Being tough gave us war in Iraq, a war that has been costly in lives and money. It was based on false premises. It was badly planned. And it included atrocities at Abu Ghraib and elsewhere that threaten our claim to the moral high ground. Being tough gave us a long and costly war in Vietnam, based on questionable origins and a problematic implementation. Intelligent flexibility brought the Cold War to an end. Modeling American values and being honest to our values made Eastern Europeans want to be like us. These values continue to make us friends and admirers in the world. In war as in politics, gender, race, and money, this book will argue that the left has always been right.

☙❧

At the start of this preface, I claimed to be presenting a "measured look" at American history. I believe that to be true. The impact of progressive ideas and progressive changes in the United States over the last two centuries is so overwhelming that conservatives have given up almost every argument they used in the past to oppose change. However, conservatives still point to the past as our model. Michelle Bachman gave us an example of that when she claimed that our founding fathers fought and struggled to end slavery. On the contrary, they wrote a constitution that accepted slavery and many founding fathers owned slaves.

Sarah Palin's take on Paul Revere gives us another example. She had him "ringing those bells," "warning the British," and telling British troops that Americans would not give up their guns. He rang no bells, he warned the American patriots rather than the British, and he had no reason to speak up for the Second Amendment, which would not be written for more than a decade. Paul Revere was in *intelligence*, gathering and passing on crucial information. That is what made his ride significant. Palin's version would have been absurd behavior, compromising both the secrecy and speed of his mission. She and her fellow activists pride themselves on being rooted in American history. Some of them even dress up in three-cornered hats, trying to resemble as well as praise the founding fathers. Palin's riff on Revere, however, illustrates the thinness and carelessness of their history. Her supporters, angry that she was the target of ridicule, then doubled down on the ignorance factor. They tried to invent and add so many changes to the Wikipedia article on Paul Revere that the site had to be shut down.

These two examples of mistaken history are part of a deeper problem. A portion of the American public has lost its hold on reality. Facts do not matter. Evidence does not matter. The idea that we should listen to experts is routinely dismissed, even if these experts have spent their highly competitive and successful lives studying some aspect of science or economics or history. The use of reasoned argument has given way to a commitment to ideology above all. If the facts, the evidence, the application of expertise, and rational analysis all point in an unwelcome direction, these elements are all ignored. It would seem beyond dispute that the attributes of the human brain and the triumphs of human reason have nurtured human accomplishment throughout history—at least since the discovery of fire and invention of the wheel, but especially since the "age of reason" took hold in the eighteenth century. For many Americans, however, these attributes and accomplishments of the human brain are thrown out with the trash. A portion of the American public has lost its mind.

I am describing rightwing conservatives, of course. There may be a version of conservatism that has not completely lost its mind, a portion of the Republican Party that pays attention to evidence and reason. But almost all Republicans in 2012 deny global warming, despite the fact that 97% of climate scientists agree that it is happening and that it is worsened by human activity, and despite the fact that these scientists have both evidence and a credible theory to support their conclusions. Many Republicans oppose Darwin's theory of evolution, or at least want American children to be taught "creationism" or "intelligent design" in science courses. That is their stance, even though creationism and intelligent design are not actually based on science. Vast areas of scientific accomplishment—in biology, genetics, and ecology, for example—could not exist without the theory of evolution.

The issues of global warming and evolution are part of a larger problem. Despite the extraordinary accomplishments of modern science, many or most Republicans will not give science their stamp of approval. That is because mindless Republicans now dictate the party's stance, with the Tea Party phenomenon as the most visible manifestation. Tea Party enthusiasts represent a small fraction of the American public. However, they now essentially control the Republican Party, including the Republican majority in the House of Representatives, because they are the least willing to listen to other points of view or compromise. Their exaggerated influence is also seen in the method we employ for selecting political candidates. The most passionate Republicans, those on the rightwing fringe, are most likely to vote in primaries. As a result, rational and educated Republicans running for office have to bow to ignorance, rather than stand up for evidence, reason, and expertise. They have to sign pledges. They have to avoid saying anything that might offend the mindless right.

The point of this book is to argue that the actual history of the United States, reality-based history, tells us things that Sarah Palin and the Tea Party do not want to hear. Consider two questions: Have we made our nation better over time? Can we solve our present problems and make our society even better in the future? Progressives are the ones who answer yes to both questions. Progressives by definition believe in progress. They believe in making full use of modern science, expertise, and the best of human reason to try to nurture a better nation and a better world. They take our American ideals of fairness, justice and equality as a guide. For two hundred years we have moved in the direction of greater fairness and justice, ending slavery, ending Jim Crow racism, and reducing gender discrimination. Progressives are proud of that. If conservatives in the past were on the wrong side and stood in the way of progressive change, why would we ever think that conservatives today have the best answers?

I am sure that about 30% of the American public will reject my claims in this book. My suggestion to those within the other 70% is that they should think twice before casting their votes for Republicans and allying themselves with the mindless right. Our greatest success as a nation has been rooted in our values of fairness, justice and equality, values which have been more and more fully realized over time. These values are good for our society. They are also good for our stature as a nation, because they are widely admired throughout the world. They represent a significant portion of our "soft" power. Our greatest success has also been rooted in our intelligence, from the wisdom of our founding fathers to the world class scholars who win Nobel Prizes today. Unfortunately, Republicans are now in thrall to the mindless 30%. Unable to control their radical right wing, if handed power they will lead us astray.

SELF-EVIDENT TRUTHS: AN INTRODUCTION

Our common starting point: "We hold these truths to be self-evident"

In the birthing process of the United States of America, the first and most important words came in the well-known and widely-quoted preamble to the Declaration of Independence: "We hold these truths to be self-evident, that all men are created equal, that they are endowed by their Creator with certain unalienable Rights, that among these are Life, Liberty, and the pursuit of Happiness." Thomas Jefferson wrote these words. The Continental Congress endorsed these words. They put them at the heart of their argument as the Thirteen Colonies claimed the right to break the bonds of British colonial control. Every American student has heard these words. Many can say these words by heart. However, these words also need some explication, since the "all men are created equal" portion was not actually taken seriously at the time.

The first problem is in the common usage of "men." We now hold as self-evident that Thomas Jefferson could have said or should have said "men and women," or perhaps "human beings." That is the meaning we attach to these words today. Unfortunately, Jefferson really did mean "men," since that was a standard assumption in the politics of his day. It is also self-evident, though it comes as a shock to some, that Thomas Jefferson owned slaves. Thus he was hardly acting out in his own life the idea that "all men are created equal." Neither was George Washington nor James Madison nor many other founding fathers who also owned slaves. We certainly do not approve of slave ownership today, but that was their reality. If we look more closely at the ideas of the founding fathers, it is also self-evident that those voting members of the Continental Congress in 1776 had no intention of extending the vote even to the already limited category of *all* white men. They simply assumed at the time that ownership of property would be the appropriate measure of who should have a political voice. In other words, well-established white men would vote and poor white men would not.

These words in the Declaration of Independence, "all men are created equal," seem quite hypocritical when we measure them against realities in the American colonies at the time. However, as a statement of the ideals of the United States that gradually developed over more than two centuries, these words stand up very well. The greatness in the story of the United States is embodied in them. Our claim to fame and our claim to admiration from other parts of the world are above all to be found in the happy fact that we steadily moved toward real equality, toward making the idealistic words in our Declaration of Independence meaningful. Thomas Jefferson and his fellow founding fathers did not live out the ideal of the words he wrote, but those words made a wonderful blueprint. Jefferson, drawing upon the Enlightenment ideas of eighteenth-century Europe, produced a set of humane values that have very nicely stood the test of time.

Educated people during the Enlightenment, people like John Locke in England and Montesquieu in France, celebrated reason and science. They believed that intelligent use of reason and science could make life better. They criticized medieval ideas of monarchy and authority and wrote about things like social contracts and the rights of human beings. Our founding fathers read the European books, picked up on the spirit of reason and science, and wrote these ideas into our national fabric. Thomas Jefferson, one of the brightest and best-educated of the lot, wrote the words of the Declaration of Independence. Over the next few years, our founding fathers wrote the social contract we still live by today. Minor modifications since then have only moved us further in the direction of those ideals to which they pointed.

As indicated above, we do not live by or admire Thomas Jefferson's *implementation* of these words. If "original intent" enthusiasts want to interpret the U.S. Constitution by the "intentions" of the founding fathers, they face a problem. They either have to advocate a set of principles that virtually no one today would accept, or they have to add a large asterisk and admit that the founding fathers were simply wrong on many of the most important things. They were wrong on democracy, they were wrong on gender, and they were wrong on race. Almost no one in today's America would countenance the retrograde ideas of those men. Fortunately, we have moved far, far beyond them, because we have changed with the times, we have accepted the ideas put forth by generation after generation of progressive reformers of our tradition. That is how we have learned to recognize the true value in the words of the Declaration of Independence. That is how we have reduced a substantial portion of the hypocrisy in those idealistic words and brought them closer to reality.

Our common ground: The left has always been right

Even the most conservative Republican in today's America would be unlikely to advocate a return to our political attitudes of 1776. None of them would openly say that white men of property are the only ones who are "created equal," the only ones with the right to "life, liberty, and the pursuit of happiness." No one outside the most radical rightwing fringe would propose taking away women's place in American democracy or their assurance of equal rights under our system. No one outside the Ku Klux Klan would advocate a return to Thomas Jefferson's practice of slavery or to the harsh, legalized racism of Jim Crow America as it existed prior to the Civil Rights Movement. American politics may seem polarized today, but, despite this polarization, almost all of us agree on the most basic principles rooted in the Declaration of Independence as we interpret them now. We hold these truths to be self-evident, that all men, all women, and all races are created equal, that all are entitled to life, liberty, and the pursuit of happiness. We believe in democracy, including one person one vote. We believe in the basic rights of women, including the right to vote and to equal treatment under the law. And we believe in the basic rights of African Americans and other minorities.

However, these common beliefs cannot hide the chasm in American politics on issues of gender and race. Most people on the right today oppose many of the most crucial issues advocated by women's groups, including equal pay for equal work, affirmative action in the workplace, the right to choose an abortion, and even sex education. Some on the right continue to think women's only proper place is in the home (in Rick Santorum's case, without contraception), and some seem happy to disparage feminists as "feminazis." Rush Limbaugh and others who use this term must not know that their point of view places them quite close to the most famous Nazi of them all, Adolf Hitler. Like them, he opposed feminism and argued that the role of women should be the traditional one of staying home and raising children. He even offered bronze, silver and gold medals to women who produced four, six, or eight children. This anti-feminist agenda represented a significant part of Hitler's appeal to traditional Germans in the aftermath of the "roaring twenties," and it seems uncomfortably close to the attitudes of those among us who think the *feminists* are the ones who are Nazis.

Despite rightwing opposition to feminism, however, and other differences over gender politics, virtually all Americans routinely accept the Nineteenth Amendment to the Constitution. Even anti-feminists on the right would never seriously try to deny women the right to vote. Few would ever deny that women should be considered full human beings, with the legal right to own property, get an education, pursue an occupation, and choose their path in life as a man would do. We do not believe that women should be denied schooling. We do not believe they should be told by law that women cannot do this or cannot do that. We do not accept the paternalistic idea that young girls of 12 should be told by their parents whom to marry. We are proud of these things. Americans left and right recognize these ideas as a proper expression of elemental fairness, a natural component of democracy and democratic values. Those few who might disagree with these basic women's rights would be placing themselves far outside the mainstream of American politics and culture.

Much the same thing can be said about race. There is a chasm in America on the politics of race. There is also a belief by leftists that some on the right encode their politics of race, slyly hinting at racial arguments and racial prejudice in an effort to attract racist voters, while feigning complete innocence and denying any racist intent. However, even if there does exist a racist undertone, no serious voice in America today advocates undoing the fundamental achievements of the Civil Rights Movement. No one would campaign to reverse Brown vs. Board of Education or overturn the Voting Rights Act of 1965. No one would deny the basic right of African Americans to vote. No one outside the Ku Klux Klan would argue in favor of apartheid in America or propose a return to "whites only" schools, lunch counters, drinking fountains, swimming pools, and park benches. Almost all Americans today see the gains of the Civil Rights Era as a proper expression of elemental fairness, a natural component of democracy and democratic values. In this case also, those few who might express disagreement would be placing themselves far outside the mainstream of American politics and culture.

Now consider this: Each of these changes—which we all now endorse and view with pride—received bitter opposition from conservatives at the time. Those on the right opposed the women's movement, just as Adolf Hitler and most other conservatives in every modernizing culture have opposed the emancipation of women. They argued from God and from nature as they tried to make sure that women's life options were kept within the narrow bounds of male-dominated practice. It was also conservatives who argued against the Civil Rights Movement. Here too they claimed that both God and nature were on their side. In both cases conservatives were trying to maintain the status quo, trying to make sure that privileges held by men and held by white people would not be reduced. There is another obvious fact about these two issues. In both cases it was progressives on the left who supported change.

The story of American ideals from 1776 until today is the story of progress we have made on Thomas Jefferson's words in the Declaration of Independence. Over time we have gradually brought his blueprint closer to reality, and we are proud of that. This required progressive reform, even wrenching reform, rather than rootedness in tradition. The very word "progressive" incorporates the optimistic belief that the world can be made a better place, that progress can occur. It includes the claim that unfair practices exist, along with the belief they can be made better. Progressives believe that our ability to implement our ideals—fairness, justice, and equal rights—can be improved. We can measure our practices against our values and find ways to bring them closer to our ideals. It is the progressive point of view, fortunately, that has been successful throughout our entire history.

The best thing we have done as a nation over more than two centuries is to take Thomas Jefferson's words seriously and make them more and more self-evident. That has made the United States a better place. We have broadened our sense of fairness and justice, and on these basic questions of change, no one today disagrees. Yet conservatives fought these changes every step of the way. The standard conservative argument, then and now, is that we can ignore leftist calls for change, because our system is not unfair. Conservatives denied that slavery was unfair. They denied that Jim Crow racism was unfair. They denied that women's legal inability to vote or get an education or, if married, to own property in their own name was unfair. By definition, conservatives in every era want to preserve the past or return to the past. They argue in favor of tradition, even though many traditions of the past now seem patently unjust. By contrast, progressives in every era believe that change toward greater fairness and equality of opportunity—even change imposed by government, if necessary—will make this a better nation, make us less hypocritical in relation to the values we claim to hold. Our success as a nation is rooted in the success of progressives. Given this patently obvious history of progressives and conservatives, why would we think that conservatives are getting it right this time? Conservatives eventually agree with the changes that are made, but never at the time.

The Left Has Always Been Right

Our common history: Definitions and themes in leftwing America

We must start with a caveat about definitions. I am dealing with left and right, not with extreme left and extreme right. Neither of the extreme versions has resulted in a heritage worth defending. The extreme left of the political spectrum brings us to communism. Communism in the twentieth century, especially the attempt to enforce economic equality according to some version of a Marxist ideal, turned out very badly. Stalin and Mao represent the worst versions of that revolutionary leftwing mode. They did not even manage to achieve their alleged goal of economic equality, and they definitely abused power, denied basic rights, and left behind a massive number of dead victims. The extreme right of the political spectrum brings us to fascism. Fascism in the twentieth century gave us a bitter lesson about what to avoid, rather than a model to follow. Hitler's version of rightwing fascism is the most famous and was the most deadly, resulting in millions of innocent dead during the Holocaust. However, fascism at any time and place opposes democracy, equality, and the basic idea of human rights, while combining nationalism, militarism, enforced inequality, and authoritarian, violent, anti-democratic government into a very nasty stew.

In this book I am assuming that most of us reject the radical and violent left, as we reject the radical and violent right. I am not claiming that rightwing Republicans in America today are fascists. I would also deny Republicans the right to call Barack Obama a Marxist, a socialist, or a communist. (Those who cross over the political spectrum and label Obama a Nazi are just proving their complete lack of historical awareness.) My point is not that conservatives in America are fascists, but simply that they are on the wrong side of history. I believe that any close look at American history in terms of the values we all accept and admire today will show that to be the case.

This book is based on the assumption that fairness, equal opportunity, and basic human rights represent the essence of the American tradition, the best of our heritage. That underlies my assessment of the progressive left. I will argue that at every step toward today's America there was a situation we now judge to have been unequal and unfair. In each case, there was a constituency which benefited from that situation—for example, from the institution of slavery, the maintenance of male chauvinism, or the continuation of Jim Crow racism. Unless they rose above their personal stake in the issue, their voices were conservative by definition. They wanted to preserve the past and hang on to a tradition. It is now absolutely clear to us that each of these situations involved an injustice, a violation of human rights, discrimination against some group based upon stereotypes about that group and justification of its mistreatment. In each case, the argument in favor of change was an argument for fairness, for justice, for the application of our concept of basic human rights.

Progressives, by definition, want to maximize fairness and justice, the equitable treatment of all groups within our nation. Any argument for change which does not involve maximizing fairness and justice does not deserve the term progressive. That might not always be apparent at a given moment. Arguments were raised about the injustice for men, the injustice for whites, the injustice for slave owners as each group lost its legally privileged position. Those arguments are now commonly seen to have been fallacious. The broader picture of fairness and equity surely falls on the side of the slaves to be freed and the women and minorities to be granted equal rights.

This book not only advocates fairness, equality, and justice, it also assumes the importance of reason. It assumes we can use our brains to interrogate history. We can look for evidence from the past and we can use reason plus evidence to thread our way through to the present. I believe it is virtually impossible to find a reasonable argument against my historical assessment presented here. I would be shocked to find any conservative arguing against the ending of slavery or the ending of legal discrimination against women and minorities. These were good changes and they were consistent with the most important of American values. My goal in this book is to lay out a rational assessment of these and other themes in American history, arguing that ultimately the left has always been right.

Chapter 1 deals with the idea of democracy. Traditionalists always got it wrong, from Loyalists who supported the legal rights of

King George III and opposed the American Revolution, to those traditionalists who opposed every increase in democratic equality. Democracy means that government should be the voice of the people. Today we have expanded our definition of "the people" and their right to a voice, but always against conservatives who wanted to keep things as they were. The second important democratic value involves protecting the rights of minorities, especially the rights to free speech, free assembly, a free press, and freedom of religion, but also the right not to be discriminated against in seeking a job, seeking a home, seeking a loan, or seeking an education. I argue that these rights also have been limited by conservatives and advocated by liberals.

Chapter 2 deals with gender. Traditionalists always opposed gender equality, because our tradition is rooted in a male-dominated, patriarchal culture. From the time of the American Revolution to the present, leftwing voices have argued for female equality. At each step of the way, conservatives put arguments and laws in the way of that equality. Chapter 3 develops similar arguments about race in America. It points out the contours of our scandalous past on racial matters. It then highlights the accomplishments brought about by the Civil War, the manner in which those accomplishments were subverted by post-Civil War conservatives, and the need for progressives a century later to undertake and support the Civil Rights Movement.

Chapter 4 deals with money. We are known as a capitalist nation. We even described the Cold War as a war between Capitalism and Communism. Without doubt, many of our greatest successes as a nation involve our success at capitalist production. This can be seen in the second half of the nineteenth century, when American resources, American industrialization, and American management techniques made us the richest nation in the world. I describe, however, the moral and human failure of "free market capitalism" by the end of the nineteenth century. The scandals of unrestricted capitalism ushered in the reforms of the Progressive Era at the turn of that century, when progressives like Teddy Roosevelt and Woodrow Wilson tried to tame capitalism for the public good. Many of those reforms are ones we would not want to do without, things such as restrictions on child labor and national regulation of food safety. In the 1930s Franklin Roosevelt introduced other important and widely accepted programs, such as the FDIC protecting our holdings in banks, and Social Security creating some dignity for the elderly and the infirm. Since the 1980s, the basic principles driving Teddy Roosevelt, Woodrow Wilson, and Franklin Roosevelt have been under attack. Conservatives in America now express their devotion to unregulated, laissez-faire capitalism in ways that disregard more than a century of experience. They demean the many programs that protect us from vulture capitalism and they ignore the lessons of history that cry out for the rational regulation of capitalism for our mutual benefit. Under the din of conservative attack, the many important accomplishments of good government have nearly disappeared from view.

Chapter 5 deals with war. Since World War II, the United States has supported a large peacetime military and been the most powerful nation in the world. This chapter looks at war and foreign policy from George Washington to George W. Bush. In particular, it discusses the difficult balancing act between maintaining our ideals and employing our ability to use raw power. We try to see ourselves as a good nation, unsullied by self-interest and seeking to promote democracy and human happiness around the globe; but we also are tempted to use our unprecedented military strength in ways that will benefit our wealth and power, even at the expense of our ideals. Other nations have done this throughout history, so we are not alone. However, our use of power does raise questions about our self-image and our appropriate stance in the world. It also raises questions about efficacy, whether our reliance on "overwhelming force" is a sure path to success.

In a concluding chapter, I assess political issues of today. This chapter is based upon the claim made throughout the book that certain American values are pre-eminent: justice, fairness, a respect for basic human rights. I recognize that various groups in American history have felt threatened by change, threatened especially by changes advocated by progressive idealists, but I argue that they have been

The Left Has Always Been Right

wrong. We should all be happy that slave owners, Jim Crow racists, and male chauvinists did not prevail. Given these lessons of history, what should a rational, well-meaning, well-informed American voter be thinking today? I suggest a simple rule of thumb to guide our thoughts: The left has always been right. We should keep that in mind so that we do not embarrass ourselves in the eyes of our children and grandchildren.

The epilogue considers a current issue—same-sex marriage—on which conservatives today are setting themselves up for embarrassment. Within a generation, children of conservatives will wonder how their parents could have been so homophobic. It will be the same as with an earlier generation of children, those who wondered how their 1950s parents could have been so racist. Conservatives are simply wrong on this issue. It is a question of civil rights and equality. It is also a question of the separation of church and state. Opponents of same-sex marriage routinely invoke religion. They point to their version of their God, rather like fundamentalist Muslims trying to impose Sharia law in places like Turkey and Egypt.

Equal rights and the ideal of secular law will eventually prevail. Very few Americans under forty oppose same-sex marriage, even as their elders echo conservatives from the nineteenth century. Conservatives opposed to same-sex marriage resemble those in the past who cited New Testament passages telling slaves to obey their masters and wives to submit to their husbands. Today's conservatives have learned either to ignore or reinterpret those Bible passages. They will eventually do that with same-sex marriage. The beauty and logic of equality and of that inspiring phrase, "all men are created equal," will again prevail. The left is right again. As in the past, however, many individuals will suffer from unequal and unfair treatment until these latest conservative arguments for inequality are brushed aside.

CHAPTER 1: DEMOCRACY

Democracy, elitism, and the right to vote

It is often forgotten that our Founding Fathers did not believe in democracy. They believed in representative government, as they had learned it from the English system of Parliament. They were ahead of the English, though, and most other Europeans in thinking they could get along without dynastic monarchy. Given their frustrations with George III, they proved ready to give up the ancient practice that arbitrarily placed the eldest son on his dead father's throne for life, with all the power and privileges appurtenant thereto. American "republicanism"—the idea of replacing hereditary monarchy with elected leaders—proved a very powerful trend. Monarchy nearly everywhere in the next century or two was either dislodged by violence, resulting in a republic, or disempowered by law, resulting in restricted, largely symbolic, constitutional monarchy. Our Founding Fathers were radical enough to defy monarchy before anyone else in modern times, but they did not believe in actual democracy.

James Madison addressed the idea of democracy in *The Federalist No. 10* with these critical words, "Hence it is that such democracies have ever been spectacles of turbulence and contention; have ever been found incompatible with personal security or the rights of property; and have in general been as short in their lives as they have been violent in their deaths." To be fair, by "such democracies" Madison meant pure democracies, small, face-to-face democracies, as found in ancient Athens. He also was defending minorities against the potential tyranny of a democracy, something he and others hoped to remedy with the first ten amendments to the Constitution, the Bill of Rights. However, Madison, as a man of considerable property and as a slave owner, was suspicious of democracy as we understand it and thought "the better sort of people" should govern.

Madison and the other Founding Fathers believed in elitism, not democracy. They represented the elite within the American colonies, the richest and the best educated, and they firmly believed that governmental authority should remain in their hands. Portraits of George Washington and other political leaders of the time tell us a lot. We can see that they dressed just like the aristocracy and monarchs of Europe. Not everyone in America at that time wore powdered wigs, frilly shirts, silk brocade coats, and white silk stockings, but our Founding Fathers did. They dressed in this style because they could afford it, and because they did not want to be mistaken for the masses. Neither did they want the masses to be the ones to control their new nation.

We can see the suspicion of our Founding Fathers toward democracy in their most carefully prepared document, the U.S. Constitution. That document in its original form placed many impediments in the path of democracy. Some were simply subsumed in the granting of powers to the individual states. For example, each state had the right to determine their qualifications for voting, and they essentially followed English practice in limiting the vote to white men with a certain amount of property. Each state also had the right to cast its electoral votes for president according to its own procedure. That meant that the first several presidents never won the "popular vote," because there was no popular vote. State legislatures selected the electors, who in turn elected the president. A similar principle determined the election of U.S. Senators, who were selected by state legislators rather than by state voters. This lasted until the Seventeenth Amendment to the Constitution, ratified in 1913.

Both the Electoral College and the indirect method for electing senators were based on a distrust of simple and direct voting. It was assumed that voters, even though narrowed by gender, wealth and race, could not be trusted to make the most important decisions. Their elected representatives within each state were expected to have more education and a better understanding about life than the average voter, thus making them more suitable for controlling the Senate and the Presidency. Another impediment to democracy can be seen in our vaunted three-branch system of government, with its checks and balances. This effectively limited the voice of the people, since only one group—the members of the House of Representatives—was elected directly by the people. Any one of the less democratically selected sectors—the Senate, the President, or the appointed Supreme Court Justices—could derail the wishes of the House, making it much harder to pass than to obstruct any piece of legislation.

If we look at how this Constitution came to be written, it helps illustrate some of the tensions between our Founding Fathers and their constituents. Our first constitution, the Articles of Confederation, written in 1777 and approved by 1781, created a nation strong enough to win the Revolutionary War against Britain. After the war, however, many of the American elite decided that the Articles of Confederation were not strong enough to create a proper nation. By 1787 representatives from the states gathered in Philadelphia with the assignment to "amend" the Articles. They decided instead to throw them out and write an entirely new document. They did this even though that meant violating their assignment and even though this decision was technically illegal. The Articles of Confederation specified that any amendment required the unanimous consent of all thirteen states, but our Founding Fathers declared that this new Constitution would go into effect if nine of the thirteen states ratified it. Nine states did ratify the Constitution by 1789, allowing the first Congress to take its seat, greeted by the first President, George Washington. By 1790 all thirteen states had ratified the Constitution, along with the first ten amendments, the Bill of Rights, and no one has seriously quibbled with the legality of the process since that time. In fact, the U.S. Constitution is much admired as the oldest, longest-lasting written constitution in the world. But it did not create democratic government as we know it today.

About one century ago Charles Beard produced a book under a title which transparently indicates his approach, *An Economic Interpretation of the Constitution of the United States* (1913). He argued the radical thesis that the Founding Fathers simply did a deal for themselves when they wrote the Constitution. One aspect of his argument involved a specific financial situation at the time, the infant national debt, and the question of who would make money if that debt were paid off. The debt itself originated when the Thirteen Colonies could not afford to pay for the American Revolution. They received a large portion of their funding from France, which was eager to see its rival England weakened. However, the Continental Congress also paid various suppliers of materials as well as soldiers in the Continental Army in pieces of paper, which promised to pay a certain amount in real money at a later time. After the war and under the Articles of Confederation, it soon was seen that these IOUs were not likely to be paid off at face value, due to the inability of the national government to raise funds and meet its obligations. Beard noted that American elites, people such as George Washington and others, had speculated in this "scrip," buying it up for pennies on the dollar. Ex-servicemen, for example, were happy to accept a few dollars in real money instead of waiting for the unlikely time when their scraps of paper would be worth the much larger amounts written on their face. After buying up these notes, speculators then required a national government strong enough to pay off the national debt and committed to doing so at face value. That would give them a windfall profit.

The new government under George Washington, with Alexander Hamilton as the Secretary of the Treasury, did in fact adopt a policy to pay off the national debt, and speculators in "scrip" did benefit. However, the *Economic Interpretation* by Charles Beard is not now widely accepted or seen as an adequate explanation for the writing of the U.S. Constitution. Too many genuine political arguments were in play in the discussions at Philadelphia to make the single explanation of economics seem convincing. But Beard's approach does prompt us to notice economic and class issues which really were in play at the time.

For example, the Articles of Confederation created no federal court system to protect the assets of the rich. When poor people in Connecticut borrowed money from bankers in New York, there was no national court to enforce their contract. If the Connecticut state legislature, responding to Connecticut voters during an economic downturn perhaps, were to declare a moratorium or write state law to absolve people from paying their debt to New York bankers, those bankers would have no recourse beyond going to a state court. A New York judge would rule in their favor, no doubt, but could not enforce that judgment in Connecticut. A Connecticut court could enforce its judgment on its citizens, but would judge according to Connecticut law. Under the Articles of Confederation, rich people who loaned money across state lines simply could not defend themselves against poor people who chose not to pay.

Another legal issue can be seen in interstate questions of land ownership. The young George Washington is well known as a surveyor. In the 1760s he launched an expedition into western portions of the Ohio Territory, surveyed the area, and made claims for the Virginia Land Company (made up of himself and other Virginia investors) on vast tracts of land. Later, pioneers moved westward and claimed portions of the same land. They did so by settling on it, building their homes, and beginning to farm. They thus seem to fit very well into our mythology of the West, a land of opportunity for the intrepid. But to land claimants in Virginia, these intrepid pioneers were merely squatters sitting on land they did not own. George Washington visited western Ohio again in 1783 and explained to those living there his legal ownership. He offered to sell, but they refused his price. He offered to let them pay rent, but they chose not to pay. In their eyes they owned the land by right of settlement and improvement. Washington and the Virginia Land Company had easily convinced the Virginia legislature to grant them legal title to the land; but under the Articles of Confederation, courts in Virginia had no authority to enforce such claims in Ohio.

The conflict between George Washington and Ohio settlers over land rights points toward a larger tension between common people and the elites at that time. Despite the careful writing of the U.S. Constitution by the elites and despite the various impediments to democracy they built into it, despite the new Federal Court system, and despite the dominance of elites during the presidencies of George Washington and John Adams, elites could not withstand the momentum they themselves had started with their rhetoric of justice and equality. The elitist party of George Washington, Alexander

Hamilton and John Adams, known as the Federalists, held the White House for a mere twelve years. John Adams lost to a representative of the "common people," Thomas Jefferson, in the election of 1800, and Federalists then simply died out as a viable political movement. Though they were in the political tradition of the revered Father of the Nation, George Washington, no Federalist ever again won the presidency.

The political career of Andrew Jackson helps illustrate these issues. He was born in Virginia, but moved to Tennessee as a young attorney. He then entered national government in 1797, as Tennessee's first congressman and soon as one of its senators. The young Jackson from Tennessee chose not to emulate the sartorial style of George Washington, who was just stepping down from his second term as President. He made no effort to fit in with proper politicians from the Eastern Seaboard. Instead of wearing a white powdered wig as he took his seat, Jackson chose to retain the unshorn, half-savage look of Tennessee, tying his long hair in back with an eel skin. Three decades later Jackson arrived in Washington as the first western president. In fact, he was the first president not from the elite states of Virginia (four presidents by then) or Massachusetts (two). He was elected president in 1828 because the elitist assumptions of our Founding Fathers had been quite drastically overturned.

Within the first generation of our nation's existence, most states changed their rules and started granting the vote to all white men, not just owners of property. States also began choosing to hold the popular vote we now recognize as the means for selecting the Electoral College. In the election of 1828, Andrew Jackson reached the White House on the basis of his popularity with the voters, not his respectability among the elite, and that led to a new phase in American politics. We still label it "Jacksonian democracy." Earlier presidents had considered themselves gentlemen and tried to dress and act accordingly. In the election of 1824, John Quincy Adams, a refined gentleman and son of a former president, won the presidency. He did so despite attracting fewer popular votes than Jackson and despite winning fewer electoral votes. Four candidates split the vote that year, so that no one secured a majority in the Electoral College. Adams then reached the White House by vote of the House of Representatives, as specified in the Constitution for such a situation. Jackson supporters were outraged at this violation of the popular will. They blamed the House vote on a "corrupt bargain" and built up their momentum for the election of 1828. In the spring of 1829, when Andrew Jackson reached Washington as the newly elected President, his friends and supporters famously held a drunken celebration in the White House. They may have spit tobacco juice on the carpet and their boisterous partying may seem to us unseemly, but the inauguration of Andrew Jackson signaled the idea of a broad and unrestricted electorate. Only women and minorities remained to be added to the rolls in order to create the democratic vote as we know it today.

Progressive steps on the American political path
Contrasting George Washington's powdered wig and Andrew Jackson's eel skin is only one way of assessing left and right in the American past, and it has the disadvantage of not taking chronology into account. The issues differed at different stages in our history and no specific behavior—getting drunk and spitting tobacco juice on the White House carpet, for example—can be labeled inherently left or right. At each turning point, however, we can assess which choice might move us in the direction of greater fairness, greater equity, and greater respect for human rights, the hallmarks of modern democracy.

If we begin with the American Revolution, we find the revolutionaries were the ones claiming their right to vote on taxes and otherwise to impact the political process. This was at a time when Members of Parliament in London and the government of George III exercised legal control throughout the British Empire. Those colonists who remained loyal to King George surely thought that law, honor, and tradition were on their side. Some of them held respected positions in the American colonies. These Loyalists (also called "Tories") made certain places, for example, New York City, dangerous for George Washington or other patriot leaders, who might have been arrested as criminals. Today, however, we justify the patriots in their inherently illegal activities—defying British law, refusing to pay taxes, dumping tea into Boston Harbor—because their cause increased fairness, justice, and access to a political voice for residents of the Thirteen Colonies. In this fight, both Samuel Adams, a somewhat rowdy rabble-rouser, and George Washington, a personally conservative man rooted in his dignity, each took the progressive side.

One generation later, in the election of 1800, George Washington's Federalist allies were pushed aside as too rooted in tradition, too wedded to the American elites, and too fond of English traditions and practices. Washington's young friend Alexander Hamilton, for example, quite liked the idea of British monarchy and the concept of the British Prime Minister and his cabinet. Washington himself saw no need for more than one political party, convinced that he and Hamilton and their fellow Federalists could represent the entire nation. Thomas Jefferson, though a member of Washington's first Cabinet, soon disagreed with various policies advocated by Washington and Hamilton and formed a new party. His supporters were known as Jeffersonians, Democratic Republicans, or even "Republicans," though now they are acknowledged to be the first Democrats. Jefferson won the election of 1800 against a Federalist, John Adams. He began to advocate more policies for the common man. He and his politics were so popular that he and two of his friends from Virginia, James Madison and James Monroe, served three successive two-term presidencies in the Jeffersonian tradition. No Federalist was ever elected president again, a complete rejection of the elitist stance ascribed to Washington and his allies. By the time of James Monroe, this tradition seemed so fully in control, so without serious opposition, that his period was labeled the "Era of Good Feelings."

Good feelings quickly disappeared, however, with the disputed election of 1824 and the arrival in the White House of John Quincy Adams. Though he did not identify as a Federalist or tie himself to that dead tradition, he was clearly the son of a Federalist and part of the American elite. Andrew Jackson, by contrast, had been born in a log cabin, a fact which soon became a political virtue and led to a series of "log cabin presidents." Whether or not they eventually became as rich as Andrew Jackson or William Henry Harrison, political aspirants recognized that roots among the common people represented an advantage for appealing to the common voter. That was part of the democratization of American politics in the Age of Jackson.

The 1830s and 1840s also saw the birth of many reform movements besides the democratization of politics. This included the first public advocacy of women's rights at the Seneca Falls Convention of 1848. It also included the first serious abolitionist movement, led by the Boston activist, William Lloyd Garrison, and by a profoundly articulate ex-slave, Frederick Douglass. Harriet Tubman, another ex-slave, worked to free slaves on the Underground Railway, even risking her own freedom by venturing back into slave territory on rescue missions. Tubman's colleague, Sojourner Truth, campaigned both for the abolition of slavery and for the rights of women. White man's democracy in the Age of Jackson did not prove kind, however, either to the rights of women or the hopes for abolition. Both remained fringe movements, with women's aspirations largely ignored and the abolitionist movement quite bitterly detested as troublemaking. Even in radical Boston, William Lloyd Garrison was not celebrated but hounded and beaten by an angry mob. Congress tried to quell growing animosity between North and South by passing a Gag Act, which banned any criticism of slavery from the floor of the House.

Another scandal of "white man's politics" in the nineteenth century involved the treatment of Native Americans. Andrew Jackson himself earned his reputation as a military hero by defeating the British at the Battle of New Orleans—the one great American victory in the War of 1812—and also as an enthusiastic fighter of Indians. Later, when in the White House, he responded to a Supreme Court decision in favor of Cherokee Indians and their right to possess land in North Carolina with his famous line, "Chief Justice Marshall has made his decision, now let him enforce it." Thus failing in his constitutional duty to enforce the law of the land, Jackson condemned the Cherokee to their "Trail of Tears," a long walk to Oklahoma with many dead as well as many tears.

It is impossible to go back and reform the behavior of Americans in the West. It may even be impossible honestly to wish away the positive results of that Westward Movement, the acquisition of all states west of the Mississippi (at the expense of Mexico as well as the native populations). Finally, any close look at English acquisition of the Eastern Seaboard and the subsequent American settlement west of the Appalachian Mountains raises the same sort of questions. White Europeans invaded the North American continent with a combination of germs and guns that destroyed the local inhabitants, and with a combination of rationalizations and self-serving principles that justified the process. In the second half of the nineteenth century, this practice changed only insofar as the United States government at each step of the way signed solemn treaties, pledging to go this far and no farther. Usually that meant that the least desirable land was left to the Indians. Then, when that land began to look desirable—in its promise of gold or wheat or otherwise—all solemn promises were broken and the Indians beaten back even further. At Sand Creek, Wounded Knee, and elsewhere, this process also included brutal massacres, sometimes under the slogan, "The only good Indian is a dead Indian."

Good Government: Teddy Roosevelt and the Progressive Era

It was easy to find things to criticize by the end of the nineteenth century. A new breed of journalist, soon labeled "muckrakers," began researching and writing in newspapers, magazines and books about various abuses. By 1881 Helen Hunt Jackson captured the shameful side of Americans moving West in the title of her book, *A Century of Dishonor*. In 1890 Jacob Riis published photos of the slums of New York under the title, *How the Other Half Lives*. These were not pretty pictures, but they awakened middle class Americans to the plight of the extremely poor in their midst. Ida M. Tarbell identified a range of illegalities and abuses by which John D. Rockefeller monopolized the oil industry in her book, *The History of the Standard Oil Company* (1904). Upton Sinclair exposed stomach-turning practices in the unregulated meatpacking industry in his book, *The Jungle* (1906).

All of these problems converged at the end of the nineteenth century, when the United States was in full transition from a rural, agricultural nation to the modern, rich, urban, industrial nation it soon became. Cities on the Eastern Seaboard, cities like New York, Philadelphia, and Boston, grew into huge metropolises; and cities in the West, places like Chicago, Cincinnati, and Minneapolis, grew from tiny settlements into robust cities within a generation. This created huge problems that completely defied the laissez-faire idea that government should not interfere in people's lives.

Consider sewage. Individual farms and small villages allow a pretty simple regimen: avoid placing your outhouse over your well. Cities, with their crowded populations and multi-story tenements, desperately needed a different approach, but it could not occur by individual choice. The use of toilets connected to sewer lines would have to be legislated if cities were not to be overwhelmed with filth and disease. This meant an elaborate plan, a revenue source, the digging up of roads, the awarding of contracts, and a set of laws insisting that no one could flout the officially-accepted requirement. This problem of filth and disease also extended beyond individual cities, since no one would want to drink water out of a river serving as the sewage outlet for a city upstream. Interference in people's lives and property became a part of our urban world. None of us would ever want to be without these changes, even though they meant forcing people to pay for expensive plumbing and forcing people to pay higher taxes.

Another simple example comes from meat production. By the turn of the nineteenth century, cattle fattened on free grass in the West could be sent by rail to Chicago, where the animals would be slaughtered and the meat processed in a factory. The end product, in the form of hotdogs, sausage, or canned meat, was then shipped by rail to urban workers in need of cheap protein. It was a great system, but Sinclair's *The Jungle* described how slaughterhouses in Chicago balanced their large desire for high profit with their minimal concern for safe and clean production. They had virtually no incentive to remove anything which fell into the vats, from sawdust to rat droppings to dead rats to human fingers and hands caught in the grinders. In prior days—before meat was raised in one place, processed in another, and eaten someplace else—customers had a chance to enter a butcher shop and observe the quality of the meat; but no worker in Brooklyn could be expected to visit and inspect a meatpacking plant in Chicago. *Caveat emptor*, the old common law protection of "buyer beware," could not be expected to work in this sort of modern economy. So Teddy Roosevelt stepped in with the Pure Food and Drug Act, combining legal requirements for safe production with an inspection system to enforce compliance. Few would want to return to the old days, before government intervention; few would want to emulate today's China, for example, with its individual managers, pressed for output, speculating on what additive for increased production might or might not prove to be lethal to customers.

These issues came to the fore as almost inevitable outcomes of the new period of industrialization. After the tumult of the Civil War and its aftermath, and after a rate of financial growth that made the United States the richest and most productive nation in the world, these problems of the modern world increasingly turned into scandals. Not only were there questions about sewage and tainted meat, but also about worker safety, living conditions, trade unions, child labor. Even Margaret Thatcher, that British advocate of an unregulated economy, referred to these nineteenth-century conditions as showing the "dark side" of capitalism. Americans also had to worry about the cleaning up of politics, which had reached an unusually high level of bribery and corruption after the Civil War. The administration of Ulysses S. Grant is known as one of the most corrupt in our history. Members of Congress were paid off with railroad stock during the scandalous *Credit Mobilier* affair of the 1870s, and the entire California legislature in that era was said to be bought and paid for by the Union Pacific Railway.

By the 1880s and 1890s, muckraking journalists identified a very wide range of problems to be solved and an extensive movement for reform swept the nation. It began with progressive politicians who tried to make changes at the state and local level. It then took over both the Republican and Democratic parties. For nearly two decades the "Progressive Era" dominated national politics, ending only when American entry into World War I redirected people's attention. Many of the changes introduced in the Progressive Era are part of our national fabric today, accepted with virtually no opposition. They were bitterly opposed at the time, of course, by conservatives.

Teddy Roosevelt was the first Progressive Era president. Elected as the Republican governor of New York in 1898, he advocated government intervention to make both politics and life in New York cleaner and less corrupt. In other words, he believed in using political change to develop more fairness, justice and equality within society. Some Republicans in New York State were not happy with their new governor, since his idealism would cost them a portion of their comfortable political and personal existence. So they developed a clever method to get rid of meddlesome Teddy, nominating him to join William McKinley on the national Republican ticket for 1900. McKinley was no meddler. Already president for one term, he had placed himself safely on the side of rich industrialists and Republican Party bosses who had put him in office. Teddy Roosevelt could not be expected to do any harm in the insignificant job of vice president; but this empty honor would get him safely out of New York, where his energy and activism were a threat to entrenched interests. The scheme fell apart when McKinley fell to an assassin in September 1901. That suddenly put Teddy's energy and reformist zeal into what he called the "bully pulpit" of the White House. At 42 he was the youngest president in American history.

Roosevelt came out of a strong progressive tradition among Republicans, even if that tradition had been lost among leaders like McKinley. Abraham Lincoln and the Republican Party of the 1850s opposed the expansion of slavery and favored things like the Homestead Act, designed to make land available to common people. Once the Civil War began, it was Lincoln and the Republican Party that forced the end of slavery. Republicans then pushed through three remarkable amendments to the Constitution. The Thirteenth Amendment in 1865 ended slavery. The Fourteenth Amendment in 1868 guaranteed citizenship to "all persons born or naturalized in the United States," with freed slaves now fully recognized as "persons." It even added this astonishing decree: "No State shall make or enforce any law which shall abridge the privileges or immunities of citizens of the United States; nor shall any State deprive any person of life, liberty, or property, without due process of law; nor deny to any person within its jurisdiction the equal protection of the laws." For good measure, the Fifteenth Amendment in 1870 added, "The right of citizens of the United States to vote shall not be denied or abridged by the United States or by any State on account of race, color, or previous condition of servitude."

These amendments (along with the *first* Civil Rights Act, the one in 1866) were so progressive that they granted freed slaves virtually all of the benefits that African Americans finally began to achieve one hundred years later! We lost an entire century of fairness, justice, and equality and we suffered a deep wound to our national honor, because progressive Republicans were unable to enforce the Reconstruction policies they had written into law. Opposed by the violence of the Ku Klux Klan, by the conservative white Democrats of the American South, and by centuries of entrenched American racism, progressive Republicans gave up on their idealism. Reconstruction failed after only a dozen years (see chapter 3 for more on the politics of race). But the Republican Party of Abraham Lincoln had begun with an extraordinary belief in progressive change imposed by government. They had vigorously pursued the goal of making the United States a fairer and more equitable nation.

In the aftermath of failed Reconstruction, there developed a rich, corporate wing of the Republican Party, much gratified by a form of politics that endorsed big business and gave rich people unrestricted freedom to make money. Presidents in the 1880s and 1890s, whether Republican or Democrat, could be relied upon to side with owners, which meant siding against the working classes and against the early stages of the trade union movement. During this era, government troops were often sent to assist corporations in breaking up strikes. This happened with state militia in the Homestead Strike of 1892 and with federal troops in the Pullman Strike of 1894. When Teddy Roosevelt became President, he turned the tables, promising a "Square Deal" for the common man.

Roosevelt accepted the idea that serious problems existed in America, and he accepted the belief that government was the only power strong enough to solve those problems. When Sinclair's *The Jungle* exposed the meatpacking industry, it convinced him that the government had a role to play. Only the national government could protect consumers around the country from tainted meat packed in Chicago, and we have had the Food and Drug Administration ever since it was created in 1907. When coal fields in Pennsylvania in 1902 experienced a bitter strike, Roosevelt chose to intervene, as had his predecessors. But he took the side of the workers, rather than the company that employed them.

Roosevelt recognized that leverage was almost entirely on the side of corporations in the early twentieth century, especially as large companies began to monopolize individual industries. So he turned to "trustbusting," breaking up the Standard Oil Company, for example. His available tool, the Sherman Antitrust Act of 1890, had previously been used against trade unions, with the idea that worker solidarity was a "restraint" on free trade in labor. Roosevelt directed his Attorney General to use the Act against large companies, taking them to court on the argument that corporate monopoly was the real enemy of free trade (for more on this see chapter 4). Roosevelt also became our first conservation president, enlisting the advice and help of Gifford Pinchot and John Muir and increasing the size and scope of our National Forests. More than any early politician, he established in the public mind the value of protecting forests and wilderness areas for future generations, despite the property rights and economic desires of those who would cut every last tree if it meant more money.

Teddy Roosevelt was popular, loved being president, and won a landslide re-election in 1904. By 1908, however, he faced a dilemma. No president had served more than two terms. He was not on course to serve two *full* terms, since he had replaced McKinley a few months after the inauguration of 1901. But Roosevelt had announced earlier that he did not think it right to violate George Washington's precedent of a two-term limit, even though he was young and fit and popular and could have tried to use the technicality that he had only been elected once so far. In 1908, despite a yearning to stay in office, TR honored his promise and limited himself to choosing and recommending a successor, William Howard Taft. Taft duly won the election of 1908 and Roosevelt went off on safari to Africa, where he shot large animals.

The next presidential election proved interesting in itself and also marked an important turning point in the history of the Republican Party. In 1912 Teddy Roosevelt could not resist his hankering to return to politics. He also had a cause, since he thought that Taft had snuggled too closely into the bosom of rich Republicans. At the Republican national convention in 1912, party bosses managed to thwart Roosevelt's widespread popularity and re-nominate Taft. Roosevelt then took his leftwing followers into a third party, widely known as the Bull Moose Party, based upon TR's claim to feel "as fit as a bull moose." This new Progressive Party split the Republican vote, which allowed Woodrow Wilson to beat long odds and become only the second Democrat in the fifty-two years since Lincoln and the Civil War to win the presidency. Many left-leaning Republican voters that year refused to vote for Taft and left the Republican Party, never to return.

Half a century later, two more nails were struck in the coffin of progressive Republicans. In the 1960s, Richard Nixon saw a chance to develop a "southern strategy." When Lyndon Johnson became president, following the assassination of John F. Kennedy, he chose to side with the justice and fairness of the Civil Rights Movement. Nixon recognized that the solid south of white Democrats could become the solid south of white Republicans. Most southern whites did in fact switch parties and, in the process, added to the conservative tilt of the Republican Party. With the election of Ronald Reagan in 1980, this rightward tilt grew stronger, and today even the policies of Ronald Reagan would not pass muster. "Liberal Republicans" and "moderate Republicans" now seem oxymoronic terms in a party in thrall to its right wing.

Shifting back to the Progressive Era, we can view the Democratic Party at that time beginning its tilt toward the left, just as Republicans dropped Teddy Roosevelt and began tilting toward the right. The progressive Woodrow Wilson, elected in 1912 by accident and safely re-elected in 1916, illustrates that the progressive swing of American voters swept across parties and briefly became the mood of almost the entire nation. In 1913 the Sixteenth Amendment to the Constitution allowed the creation of a national income tax, based on the progressive principle that those with more money benefit from and can better afford to contribute to the national good. The Seventeenth Amendment, also ratified in 1913, took the selection of Senators away from state legislators and put it in the hands of voters. Wilson also pushed for the Clayton Antitrust Act and the Federal Trade Commission, both of which pushed back the boundaries of laissez-faire.

It was only World War I, entered by the United States in 1917, that diverted national attention from the widely-accepted goals of progressivism to the needs of war. In the aftermath of that war, especially its messy peacemaking process, Wilson's progressive legacy lost its power and Warren G. Harding won the White House for Republicans by promising a "return to normalcy." His normalcy included the Teapot Dome scandal, perhaps the most brazen example of financial corruption in presidential history, and then the statement by his successor, Calvin Coolidge, that "the business of America is business." Harding, Coolidge and Herbert Hoover put their pro-business, anti-progressive, laissez-faire stamp upon American politics for twelve years, until the worst depression in American history cost Hoover his hopes for re-election in 1932—after his turn toward anti-laissez-faire measures proved too little and too late. Those twelve years of conservative Republican policies represented a short interval between the bipartisan progressivism of Teddy Roosevelt and Woodrow Wilson and the Democratic progressivism soon introduced by Teddy's distant cousin, Franklin D. Roosevelt.

Good Government: Franklin D. Roosevelt and the New Deal

The second President Roosevelt is ranked by many alongside George Washington and Abraham Lincoln as one of the three greatest presidents in American history. Some even argue that he is the greatest president of all. A standard measure of presidential greatness involves the significance of challenges successfully overcome. Washington not only led the Thirteen Colonies through the Revolutionary War, he successfully led the nation for two full terms through the birthing process of our constitutional system of government. Lincoln led the nation through its most bloody and most existential crisis, the Civil War. Franklin Roosevelt faced down our nation's worst ever economic crisis, the Great Depression, and then he successfully led the nation through our largest and most difficult military conflict, the Second World War. Roosevelt not only succeeded in the face of these two massive crises, he also took the unprecedented step of running for and winning four successive terms in office. In the process, he and his policies dominated the political landscape for at least half a century.

FDR did not run for president with an agenda for dramatic change. However, between his election in November 1932 and his inauguration in March, the national economic crisis continued to spiral out of control. The bank crisis, for example, though it involved genuine problems in bank solvency, was exacerbated by panic. Whenever rumors circulated that a bank might be in trouble, the next morning a line might stretch around the block, with customers clamoring to withdraw their money. It is literally impossible for any bank to withstand a "run on the bank." They simply cannot keep enough cash on hand to pay off more than a tiny fraction of their customers on any given day. It is in the nature and essence of a bank that it take most of the money deposited by its customers and give it to others. It does so in the form of investments, such as mortgages, so that the bank makes a rate of return large enough to pay interest on savings accounts, provide various banking services, and still hope to make a profit. This natural flaw in banks, and their need for customer confidence, led to the essential collapse of the entire banking system. By early 1933, 80% of the states had closed all banks, with no plans for what to do next and no end to the crisis in sight.

Roosevelt recognized that the banking crisis could be solved only by federal government intervention. He declared a national "bank holiday," inspiring enough confidence so that depositors dropped their panicked mentality. Then he created the real solution, the Federal Deposit Insurance Corporation or FDIC. This pro-active, government-created insurance system spread the risk, guaranteed individuals that their funds would be protected, no matter the fate of their individual bank, and solved the problem at one stroke. Since FDR intervened in banking in 1933, no customers have lost their money and no bank has gone under due to the panic of depositors! Free market capitalism completely failed to solve this problem, but intelligent government intervention solved it in a stroke.

Everybody accepts the FDIC today and nobody would want to do without it. Government intervention was the brilliant answer to the bank crisis. Franklin Roosevelt also created Social Security, a brilliant idea for pooling our national resources in order to provide some measure of comfort to the elderly and the disabled. We tinkered with Social Security in 1986 and might do so again, as greater longevity and the bubble of a postwar population boom converge and put some strain on the system. But Social Security represents an incredible success. It has added dignity and comfort to generations of the elderly, many of whom would be entirely indigent without it. This is a safety net no one but the most hard-edged, free-market ideologue would want to remove.

Under Harding, Coolidge, and Hoover, Republican orthodoxy would not accept the FDIC or Social Security. Their ideology of laissez-faire meant leaving business alone, on the assumption that the free market would solve its own problems. The bank crisis proved without question that Roosevelt's alternative view was correct, that certain forms of government intervention can solve problems, especially at times of panic and in extreme circumstances. The rest of the New Deal involved other forms of intervention, including the creation of many government jobs. Programs such as the Civilian Conservation Corps (CCC) and the Works Progress Administration (WPA) were designed to attack the crisis of unemployment, a crisis which reached 25%, the highest level of unemployment in our history. Taken together, unemployment and underemployment (shorter hours and reduced pay) also reached the highest level in our history at 50%.

Government jobs put large numbers of people to work. They also represented an investment in the future, with massive programs such as the Tennessee Valley Authority providing irrigation and electricity to a vast swath of the American South, and the Grand Coulee Dam project creating both huge agricultural opportunities and cheap electricity for the benefit of the Pacific Northwest. Workers in the CCC planted trees and built hiking trails in national parks. WPA workers built bridges and painted murals. The program even included work for songwriters like Woody Guthrie. These government jobs gave employment and hope to millions of unemployed Americans who had been in the depths of despair over an economy that had grown worse and worse for four long years. These jobs also pumped money into the economy when that was desperately needed (see chapter 4 on money). Conservative, laissez-faire politics left the unemployed without jobs and without hope. Franklin Roosevelt gave them both. No wonder an entire generation of Americans worshipped FDR, voted for FDR, and placed his portrait in their homes.

Good Government: Lyndon Johnson and the Great Society
The third major period of progressive change in the twentieth century came in the 1960s under the presidency of Lyndon Johnson. Many look back upon Johnson and his Great Society as if it was wrongheaded or a failed experiment. They are mistaken. He oversaw two massive changes in American life we would not want to be without. The first of these was in civil rights. That came as a shock to many, since John Kennedy added LBJ to his ticket in 1960 as an attempt to appeal to conservative white Democrats in the South. After Kennedy's assassination, it did not seem likely that a longtime Senator from Texas would ally with the Civil Rights Movement and make it his special issue.

Kennedy had become very popular among African Americans for the sympathy and respect he showed them, though he accomplished relatively little. He worried about offending white southern voters and he failed to get much legislation past the congressional barrier of Republicans and conservative Democrats. Johnson, however, managed to push civil rights legislation through Congress, calling it a tribute to Kennedy at that emotional moment in the aftermath of his assassination. These accomplishments included the Civil Rights Act of 1964, which outlawed discrimination by employers against blacks (and women) and banned racial segregation in places of public accommodation. He also added the Voting Rights Act of 1965, which mandated federal intervention to protect the rights of black voters in six problematic southern states. These changes represent the most important steps toward racial equality since the ending of slavery in 1865. No one would want to turn back the clock on these monumental changes. Lyndon Johnson stands alongside Martin Luther King, Jr., the NAACP, and the Civil Rights Movement as a whole. He provided the main governmental component in the engine of change.

It is important to note the personal and political courage Johnson displayed in his advocacy of civil rights for Black Americans. In August 1964, nine months after he had ascended to the presidency and revealed his advocacy of civil rights, he faced a particularly difficult issue at the Democratic National Convention in Atlantic City. Two groups of delegates arrived from Mississippi, a state where three civil rights workers had been murdered just two months previously by members of the Ku Klux Klan. One delegation, all white, had been selected in the normal southern manner at precinct meetings where blacks were refused entry. The Mississippi Freedom Democrats, formed in April 1964, claimed that they were sending the only legal delegation, since they were the ones who had followed party rules against discrimination. The resulting compromise pleased no one. Mississippi Freedom delegates were granted two seats and two at-large votes. The 24 all-white delegates held their voting rights, so long as they agreed to sign a pledge to support the party ticket in November. Twenty of those delegates refused to sign the pledge and went home, representing a first trickle in what was to become a flood.

By 1968 the Democratic Party more carefully enforced its policy against racial discrimination in the selection of delegates. White southern Democrats responded by joining "Democrats for Nixon" that year, or by supporting George Wallace. The latter's pro-segregationist candidacy won the electoral votes of five states in the deep South. Nixon Democrats and Wallace Democrats then became part of the wholesale trek into the Republican Party that soon occurred. The very fact that Lyndon Johnson, a southern Democrat, presided over these changes in black civil rights meant he was reviled as a traitor by many. It may also account for some of the disparagement of LBJ and the Great Society still widespread on the right.

The second reason for rightwing disparagement of Johnson's record is based on his "War on Poverty." He did not invent Social Security, which originated with Franklin Roosevelt and the New Deal. Much of the rest of our social safety net, however, developed under the leadership of LBJ. Inspired by Michael Harrington's book, *The Other America* (1962), progressives in the 1960s recognized that poverty in the United States had not disappeared with postwar prosperity. Rather, it continued among many groups as a deep and systemic problem. One of those groups was the elderly. Half of those over 65 had no medical insurance, so Johnson responded with Medicare. He also created Medicaid to help the poor under 65.

Despite arguments over funding levels, both Medicare and Medicaid have been a vital and accepted part of American life for half a century. Johnson also pushed the Food Stamp Act of 1964, reducing the problem of hunger and malnutrition. He created Head Start, one of his most successful interventions in education; and he passed the first legislation allowing federal aid to education, including work-study programs for college students and other forms of aid still widely accepted. Finally, Johnson created both the National Endowment for the Arts and the National Endowment for the Humanities. Taken altogether, this was one of the most active periods of legislation in American history, and it resulted in programs deemed vital half a century later. It is also important to note that Johnson actually lowered the poverty level during his term in office. In other words, his "War on Poverty" was winning. That stands out, since the poverty level has crept back up and the gap between rich and poor has dramatically increased in subsequent decades.

Johnson inaugurated his Great Society while fighting the Vietnam War, part of his policy of "guns and butter" (see chapter 5 on war for more on this topic). It seemed like he was a spendthrift at the time, and he has been reviled by some ever since as the quintessential "tax and spend" Democrat. The figures are surprisingly friendly to his legacy, however. He increased the national debt by only $54 billion, which amounted to a 17.5% increase in 5 years. This looks quite attractive in comparison to our most profligate president, Ronald Reagan, who nearly tripled the national debt. He added $1.76 trillion, about thirty times the dollar figure on Lyndon Johnson's ledger and an increase in the debt of 189% in eight years. George H.W. Bush added 55% to the debt in four years ($1.5 trillion) and George W Bush nearly doubled the debt, pushing it 86% higher in his eight years ($4.9 trillion). This is not to mention the disastrous level of fiscal imbalance he left for Barack Obama. By contrast, Bill Clinton raised the debt only 37% in his eight years ($1.54 trillion). More importantly, he *reduced* the debt as a share of GDP and he left the second President Bush with a budget surplus. It was projected to pay off the entire national debt within a decade! Taken together, Reagan, Bush I, and Bush II added $8.16 trillion to the national debt in less than three decades, representing nearly 80% of the $10.627 trillion debt handed to Barack Obama. These irrefutable figures are worth keeping in mind when Lyndon Johnson and other progressives are accused of being profligate and conservatives are considered fiscally responsible. The numbers tell a very different story.

A Final Element: Minority Rights in a Democracy

Our present variation on Jefferson's words, "all people are created equal," might be as good a definition of democracy as we can find. Furthermore, the United States has made great progress over two centuries in taking these words seriously, though it remains a work in progress. One portion of this story is simply our gradual democratization of political rights, a development that is now accepted almost without controversy. We have the right to vote, whether rich or poor, male or female, black, white, brown, red, yellow, or any color in between. That is a good thing and represents progress.

The story of American progress also involves "good government," the use of government to make this a better nation. This part of the story can become controversial, especially for those whose ideology says government is the enemy. Very few, however, want to get rid of the progressive government programs on which we rely: Social Security, the FDA, the FDIC, the SEC, the EPA, Head Start, Pell Grants, work-study. The list goes on. It is our government that enforces certain standards of safety, fairness and justice. It was the government that attacked the scandal of racial segregation in the

1960s. Many people misunderstand, take for granted, or ignore these tremendous benefits of good government. A nice illustration of the problem occurred in 2009 when an anti-government Tea Party activist at a town hall meeting said, "Just don't let the government get its hands on my Medicare!" As this shows, even Medicare—obviously a government program!—is taken for granted by many of those Americans who claim that "big government" is the source of all evil.

Minority rights represent a third element in the gradual democratization of America, and here we sometimes find a higher level of disagreement and emotion. Despite the success of the Civil Rights Movement, racial differences remain contested, as do gender issues. It is important to remember, however, that democracy without minority rights is simply not recognizable as democracy. Consider the Nazi regime in Germany. It came to power legally and democratically, though without a majority. It then got rid of democracy, but the regime almost certainly enjoyed majority support throughout most of its existence. Some of the worst Nazi policies, including the persecution of Jews and other minorities, probably would have been approved by a democratic vote of all Germans. This example points toward a broader truth: "Voice-of-the-people" democracy provides absolutely no inherent protection for minorities. By contrast, as we Americans learned to "hold these truths to be self-evident, that all men are created equal," we gradually realized that we had to remove unequal treatment across the boundaries of gender and race. Another boundary involves religion. The history of religion and democracy in America is worth a closer look.

Are Muslims created equal? It is common knowledge that the United States through at least the nineteenth century did not practice true religious freedom and remained under the control of WASPs. If you were not a white, Anglo-Saxon Protestant before the twentieth century, you need not consider running for high office, applying to a top university, or joining an important social organization. Irish Catholics, Russian Jews, and Chinese Buddhists all fell outside the equal rights promised to all. John Kennedy broke through a portion of that barrier when he was elected president in 1960, despite a certain number of voters who would never vote for an Irish Catholic. Most of the legal restrictions and many of the social prejudices have disappeared during the past century. But a variation on the problem, the question of whether the United States is a "Christian nation," seems to be alive and well. Most recently this has included self-described Christians denying various rights to Muslims in America, including the right to build places of worship.

The First Amendment includes the statement, "Congress shall make no law respecting an establishment of religion, or prohibiting the free exercise thereof." The Fourteenth Amendment put states under this umbrella, denying them the right to "abridge the privileges or immunities" of citizens or deny "equal protection of the laws." These two amendments are the source of our separation of church and state. In cases heard in 1962 and 1963, the U.S. Supreme Court banned organized prayer and Bible reading in public schools. Some on the right continue to see this as a violation of their rights, not to mention a victory for Satan.

We might not be able to determine Satan's preferences, but it is quite easy to see why democracy and the ban on prayer in public schools fit together. First of all, no individual is denied the right to pray in school; it is only a ban on public prayer and Bible reading arranged or supported by the school. Real equality in a real democracy simply cannot privilege the members of one religion over another, in school or otherwise. No person should have fewer rights or less respect before the law on the basis of holding a minority religious belief, though that routinely occurred in earlier times. Keep in mind that the former policy of prayer in public schools was specifically designed to promote Christian practice and Christian beliefs. No Jewish or Muslim child was treated equally by that practice. Furthermore, no watered-down version designed not to offend a Jew or a Muslim could avoid offending a child of some other religious belief, or a child with no religious belief at all. If we accept the basic truth that a democratic society should not privilege one among several religions—and that seems impossible to deny—then any public form of support for one religious point of view is unacceptable.

Conclusion

American history has seen the political left prevail step by step against privilege and prejudice, and that is a good thing. Our democracy is based upon equal treatment before the law, with no privilege attached to gender, race, religion, or ethnicity. Almost all violations of that principle in our past are now condemned. Our political history also includes a necessary and widely accepted increase in the size and scope of government. The Progressive Era, the New Deal, and the Great Society used good government to make changes in America that virtually no one would want to relinquish. Very few today would advocate strip mining Yellowstone or cutting down the last tree in Yosemite. Even extreme libertarians happily accept government protection against E-coli. Grand Coulee Dam and the Tennessee Valley Authority have been regional engines for prosperity hard to wish out of existence; the FDIC remains a form of national insurance for everyone with a bank account; and Social Security has been called the "third rail" of American politics, precious to the vast majority, even though it violates the avowed principles of the hard right in almost every respect. Medicare, Medicaid, Head Start, federal support for education, food stamps for the very poor, and the legal enforcement of civil rights as established by Lyndon Johnson are also progressive changes very few would want to tear from our national fabric.

There is a natural reason why government has grown over the last century. It is based on the lessons of sewage in big cities and the danger of tainted meat writ large. The modern world is extraordinarily complex, with problems unknown to our Founding Fathers. We have learned to apply their idea of fairness, equality, and justice in ways they never imagined, yet true to their principles. In fact, we are now more true to their principles than they were. The trick for modern America is to look at these changes honestly. That pretty much requires our recognition that the left has always been right. Those who stepped along the best path were following a progressive agenda as we understand it today. Our task is to be aware of this reality, not blind to it, and to use our best intelligence as we try to stay on that same path.

CHAPTER 2: GENDER

Patriarchy is wrong

Patriarchy is our past, almost universally. It is hard to find matriarchal societies, ones in which women actually rule. We have occasional exceptions, as seen in the stories of Boadicea, Joan of Arc, Queen Elizabeth I, or Catherine the Great, and we have dim legends of amazons. We have anthropological awareness of matrilineal societies, where family identity runs through the mother; and we know of matrilocal societies, where couples move in with the wife's mother. Some early American Indian cultures seem to have included a more powerful role for women in decision-making than Europeans could imagine at the time. But the pattern of the past we know best has always been patriarchal, putting men in charge. It is not a pretty picture—but it *is* a picture defended by conservatives at every grudging step in our welcome path toward change.

The pathology of patriarchy is quite clear. It gives men power and men regularly abuse that power. Take the double standard in sex, for example. The assumption has been very deep-seated within our culture that men can get away with what they want, but women must be pure. We have the Victorian idea that women were either virgins, thus eligible for marriage and motherhood, or harlots, thus available for sex. We have the mythology of the antebellum woman in the South, placed upon a pedestal of purity and honor, while mulatto children mysteriously proliferated on the plantation. This southern example is almost a textbook case of what men do when they can. Two legal categories spring to mind. First of all, we should call the practice of white men fathering mulatto children what it was—rape, since slave women could not say no. We know it happened often, since the evidence of interracial children presents as clear a body of evidence as any judge could require. Naturally, no judge at the time gave an opinion, for such cases did not end up in court.

The other legal category to consider involves miscegenation—sex across racial boundaries. States in the antebellum South (while still colonies) made miscegenation illegal almost as soon as race-based slavery developed as an institution; but that did not stop white men from practicing miscegenation. Why write the laws? First of all, it gave white men a strong motive—alongside the threat of marital discord—to deny fatherhood. Denial of paternity to avoid admitting a crime provided one more incentive among several to break the normal bond between father and child, thus leaving the slave child without a father's protection. The second reason for miscegenation laws lay in the opportunity for differential enforcement. White men who slept with black women were winked at or admired. Black men who slept with white women were punished by the full weight of the law in court—unless, of course, they were simply lynched.

Outside our particularly brutal history of a racial double standard, our sexual double standard was usually enforced by whispering, by stigma, and by shame. Our religious principles tend to be gender neutral, condemning adultery and promiscuous sex by either men or women. But our social practice placed almost the entire weight of condemnation on women. If we push back earlier in our own culture, or if we look at other patriarchal cultures, we find the double standard enforced by the stoning to death of women caught in adultery or of daughters and sisters who "dishonor" the family, while no such male corollary existed. Patriarchal practice can also include female genital mutilation—a practice designed to make it difficult or impossible for young women to have sex, as well as to try to stifle their pleasure in the act. Western Europeans invented the chastity belt for the same purpose, a contraption that can sometimes be seen in museums alongside other implements of medieval torture.

Anxiety about paternity is almost certainly the cause of the double standard in sex. Identifying the mother of a child is pretty easy. Identifying the father was always less certain, at least until DNA testing became available. Presumably men wanted to know the child was theirs, not only as assurance that they possessed the mother's loyalty and affection, but also to avoid passing on their influence and their worldly goods to another man's offspring. Cuckoldry is one of the greatest shames in any patriarchal culture. The alternative to the shamed cuckold is the preening, boasting, and posturing man. Surely these latter behaviors are deeply rooted in patriarchal ideas of sexual ownership and sexual success.

An even darker side of patriarchy can be found in male violence against women. It is true that very occasionally a woman might batter a man, murder a man, or, in sensational cases, dismember a man. However, gendered violence almost always involves men raping women, men assaulting women, and men murdering women. These stories fill our news. They have made Nancy Grace a fixture on television. Even when the crime involves kidnapping or pedophilia, it is virtually always a story about men as perpetrators. Male violence against women infiltrates our entertainment as well as our news. It is likely to find its way into some corner of the plot line of nearly every television drama or Hollywood film. It represents a prominent hook in the sex and violence gambit that sells books, sells magazines, and puts butts in the seats at the cinema. All of this male violence can only be understood as the extreme—but not entirely surprising—version of the patriarchy that conservatives always endorsed.

The end of patriarchy

We are a long way from making our world safe for women. However, progressive change has quite dramatically changed our attitudes, if not all of our practices. The nature of modernity and the logic of democracy have both played a huge role in these changes that are now so widely accepted, most of which involve an abandonment or rejection of the patriarchal model. Our trajectory since approximately the eighteenth century is quite clear. Part of the story involves our modern, urban economy and its new opportunities for women, producing changes in gender relationships that now seem like virtually inevitable outcomes of the industrial revolution. Modern industrial development depended on widespread urbanization, because industry required the concentration of a working population, transportation networks, bankers, lawyers, and various other services. Living in cities brought a huge array of changes for women in tow. Another part of the story involves the triumph of democracy, with its inherent ideal of fairness and its support for individual rights. We do not know everything about gender relationships over past millennia. But we do know that patriarchy was widespread in the traditional, authoritarian past. We also know that in our modern, urban, democratic world it is increasingly in bad odor, despite its lingering attraction to many on the right.

The urban/rural split mentioned above is ancient, of course, and almost entirely economic in its underpinnings. Human beings lived in small villages and worked at agriculture when they did not have the skill or opportunity to do anything else. That is not to say farming is a small or insignificant skill. The agricultural revolution some 10,000 years ago rescued humans from their hunter/gatherer economic mode and gave them a more secure diet. It also allowed them to live in permanent homes with increased levels of comfort, rather than as seasonal nomads, packing all their possessions with them as they followed their food supply. The agricultural revolution came about when humans learned how to plant seeds, harvest crops, and domesticate animals.

The invention of farming was a revolutionary advance. But we call it "civilization" when those same humans learned to live in cities. First of all, this change required surplus agricultural production. Those who lived in cities could then purchase food from the countryside, while they worked at a range of new skills, including reading and writing. These urban residents learned to practice—and make a living from—politics, religion, science, economics, music, literature, and art. That was the foundation for human advancement. Urban development gave us entire civilizations in places like Mesopotamia, Egypt, Greece, and Rome, as well as China, India, and elsewhere. These civilizations in their complexity and accomplishments put the simple tasks of the farmer in the shade, even though the excess production of the farmer made it all possible.

In the aftermath of 5000 years of urban life, we now have two or three centuries of *modern* urban life. It was only with the industrial revolution and the development of modern technology that the urban/rural relationship tilted entirely in the direction of urban dominance. Only the modern period has seen a tiny fraction of the population able to produce enough food for everyone else, and only modern methods of factory production have made possible the extraordinary availability of those consumer goods that have transformed our lives. We can measure "modernization" by noting when a nation tipped its balance from a primarily rural to a primarily urban population. That happened in the United States at about the end of the nineteenth century, when we became the richest nation in the world; and it happened in similar fashion for the rest of the world's richest nations. Farmers still make it all possible. Furthermore, farmers today are part of the modern, technological story, with fantastic increases in production based upon large machines and complex science. In colonial America, some 80% of the population produced food. Today perhaps 4% of the population produces food, and it does so in such great abundance that we feed other portions of the world as well as ourselves. That is what farmers give us. Cities give us bicycles and automobiles, washing machines and refrigerators, televisions and computers, smart phones and the Internet.

Cities also gave us the "new woman," for urbanization had a huge impact on gender roles. Women as well as men moved to cities. They gradually became cogs in an economy where gender made less and less difference. At first the process was quite exploitative. When machines began to do the heavy lifting, women could push buttons, turn levers, or guide product as well as men. Furthermore, cultural assumptions meant that owners felt comfortable paying women far less than men. (Another variation on the same principle soon had factory owners employing little children, the cheapest workforce of all.) But the modern economy also created a growing middle class. Alongside urbanization, the growth of a middle class represents another major indicator of a modern, successful, rich nation. Virtually all of the changes in the economy required brains as well as muscle, white collar workers as well as blue collar. For women, that first meant jobs as secretaries and telephone operators. But a modern economy needs an incredible array of auxiliary workers: bankers and lawyers, insurance agents and accountants, newspaper reporters and public relations flacks. It requires scientists, engineers, inventors, and systems analysts, plus the teachers necessary to teach all of these newly-required skills, from kindergarten through high school, from institutes of technology to research universities. As we know and now universally recognize, women can do all of these jobs as well as men.

The life we lead today was impossible in a rural, farming society. From jet travel to cocooning with our favorite DVD or movie download, from social networking to vacations in Italy or France, the world we live in was transformed by urbanization and the modern economy. So were the lives of women. The percentage of women who marry by eighteen and produce eight or ten children is now minuscule, though that used to be a common pattern. The pattern made sense on a farm. Children came naturally. They were cheap. They could perform useful chores from a very young age. That economy required no expensive education for children, from the right preschool to give them a good start to the right university, whatever the cost. Modern women marry later. That happened partly because they had the independence of a job in the city, a job which meant they no longer were financially dependent on their father until they got married and on their husband afterwards. By the 1920s, many women parlayed this financial independence into social and cultural independence. Delayed marriage also occurred because modern women spent more time acquiring an education and building a career of their own. Quite naturally these changes restricted the number of children they would produce. All of these things go together. No modern, urban society has a female population that retains the life patterns of the rural past. Urban housing is too tight, education too expensive, the woman's income too necessary, and the modern woman's claim on an equal life too great.

Democracy represents the second great change for women in the modern world. As discussed earlier in this book, the idealistic thought that "all men are created equal" virtually demands that we take "all" seriously (even though we still find that somewhat difficult when we are in the full grasp of our ethnocentricity). It also demands that we define the word "men" in its generic sense, meaning all men and women. Once we make that leap—as we did officially in 1919, when American women were granted the vote—it is hard to tell women they cannot be admitted to medical school or pursue a career in the military or run for president. Virtually all of the changes for women that develop naturally in a modern, urban economy have the added benefit of being entirely consistent with our democratic ideals. That is why we call the dissenters male chauvinists, a term of reproach. They are fighting against history, against the realities of our modern world, and against the principles of democracy we all claim to hold dear. If they happen to have a wife or a daughter, they also are likely to be waging a futile struggle. Some men, of course, still lock their women up at night. Extreme cases make the news, but these men do not earn our admiration.

Steps on the path to progressive change (Steps on the feminist path)

These changes in the modern woman have faced the disapproval—or even the wrath—of conservatives every step of the way, no matter how logical and appropriate they might seem today. That is because they challenged such a long and deep-seated tradition. Abigail Adams famously requested of John Adams as he departed for the Constitutional Convention that he "remember the ladies," though he and his colleagues did not. In England a short time later Mary Wollstonecraft gave birth to Mary Godwin Shelley, who later gave us *Frankenstein*. But this grandmother to *Frankenstein,* Mary Wollstonecraft, also was mother to modern feminism, with her book, *A Vindication of the Rights of Woman*. It was half a century later when the first political attempts in the United States to give women equal rights developed under the leadership of individuals like Elizabeth Cady Stanton and Lucretia Mott.

Many of these feminist pioneers developed their ideas within the crucible of the anti-slavery movement. Mott and Stanton traveled to London in 1840 for the World Anti-Slavery Convention, where they were stunned to be told they could not participate. As women they were only allowed to sit in a gallery above and watch the proceedings. Other women in the anti-slavery movement suffered similar indignities. Sarah and Angelina Grimké, two sisters from

South Carolina, brought their knowledge of slavery to meetings in the North, where they spoke movingly about the grim reality of slavery. When some men objected to the very idea that women would speak in public, they realized they had to take up the cause of women as well. Sojourner Truth, an ex-slave, made the rounds of the antislavery circuit during the 1840s and likewise recognized the connection between the plight of slaves and of women. When she attended a women's conference in Akron in 1851, she displayed the strong bicep in her right arm, described the hard work she had done all her life, and called out repeatedly, according to one eyewitness, "And ain't I a woman?"

The first Women's Rights Convention met in Seneca Falls, NY in 1848, under the leadership of Elizabeth Cady Stanton and Lucretia Mott. With both men and women in attendance, this group crafted a "Declaration of Sentiments," quoting the Declaration of Independence almost word for word in order to highlight the particular injustice accorded to women in a nation which had long before professed such high ideals. As with the Declaration from 1776, they justify the need for such a statement: "When, in the course of human events, it becomes necessary for one portion of the family of man to assume among the people of the earth a position different from that which they have hitherto occupied, but one to which the laws of nature and of nature's God entitle them, a decent respect to the opinions of mankind requires that they should declare the causes which impel them to such a course." The statement then goes on to make one tiny modification to the following, familiar words: "We hold these truths to be self-evident: that all men *and women* are created equal; that they are endowed by their Creator with certain inalienable rights; that among these are the right to life, liberty, and the pursuit of happiness; that to secure these rights governments are instituted, deriving their just power from the consent of the governed." Then, sticking to the format of its famous model, this Declaration of Sentiments goes on to say, "The history of mankind is a history of repeated injuries and usurpations on the part of man toward woman, having in direct object the establishment of an absolute tyranny over her. To prove this, let facts be submitted to a candid world."

The rest of the Declaration approved by the Seneca Falls Convention spoke to an agenda that continued to drive the women's movement, to a certain extent even to today. In terms of woman's right to vote, "He has never permitted her to exercise her inalienable right to the elective franchise. He has compelled her to submit to laws, in the creation of which she had no voice." This statement complained that a married woman "loses all right to property, even to the wages she earns." And speaking of those wages, "He has monopolized nearly all the profitable employments, and from those she is permitted to follow, she earns but a scanty remuneration." Furthermore, "He has denied her the facilities for obtaining a thorough education—all colleges being closed against her." (Oberlin College, the one exception, opened its doors and awarded the first bachelor degrees to women in 1841.) With regard to the double standard, "He has created a false public sentiment, by giving to the world a different code of morals for men and women, by which moral delinquencies which exclude women from society, are not only tolerated but deemed of little account in man." Finally, in words that resonate powerfully to this day, "He has endeavored in every way that he could to destroy her confidence in her own powers, to lessen her self-respect, and to make her willing to lead a dependent and abject life." The conclusion drawn from these various complaints was strong indeed:

> Now, in view of this entire disfranchisement of one-half the people of this country, their social and religious degradation,—in view of the unjust laws above mentioned, and because women do feel themselves aggrieved, oppressed, and fraudulently deprived of their most sacred rights, we insist that they have immediate admission to all the rights and privileges which belong to them as citizens of these United States.

When Elizabeth Cady Stanton, Lucretia Mott, Sarah and Angelina Grimké, and Sojourner Truth advocated for the rights of women in this manner alongside their opposition to slavery, it was natural and appropriate in terms of freedom from discrimination and equality of rights. Politically, however, the feminist side of this agenda could not compete with the enormity of the slavery issue, an issue that led to heightened violence in the 1850s and to war in 1861. Feminist concerns were inevitably pushed aside for the greater battle. From the Civil War through Reconstruction, women's rights remained mostly on the sideline. Gradually, however, a tenacious women's movement reasserted itself. This time, led by Susan B. Anthony and others in a new generation, the movement focused more narrowly on the right to vote, rather than other examples of injustice. Their strategy assumed that women earning the right to vote would lead to women earning other rights as well. Though that fond hope developed slowly, it ultimately proved true.

Wyoming Territory granted women the right to vote as early as 1869, the first of several Western locales to open this door. Nationally, however, the right to vote came only with the passage of the Nineteenth Amendment in 1919, a change that followed three-quarters of a century of work by women activists and also received a final push from World War I. The war effort did not invent the many changes for women already in motion, but it did accelerate things such as the migration of women from rural towns to large cities in search of work. Participation in a major European conflict meant that war goods had to be produced at a time when large numbers of men had left their jobs to join the military. Therefore, patriotism coupled with national need to give women both the incentive and the ability to step into many roles previously held primarily by men. After the war, grateful men were inclined to accept the suffragists' claim that women who helped their nation win the war deserved a place in their nation's voting booth. This trifecta for women—the progress of democratic ideals, the impact of suffragist activism, and the participation of women in war industries—led to women also receiving the right to vote in England, Germany and other European countries in the aftermath of the war.

A period of widespread change for women followed quickly on the heels of women's suffrage. Most of what happened in the 1920s, the era of the "flapper," was simply an intensification of earlier trends. Urbanization, new jobs for women in the industrial economy, and the burgeoning middle class with its white collar jobs for women all brought social and cultural change in their wake. However, the impact of World War I and the reality of women gaining the right to vote intensified the pace of change for women and added a distinctively feminist edge to the "Roaring Twenties." This period included a sexual revolution, for example, in which sex was discussed more openly and women began to challenge the double standard. At the same time the first synthetic materials led to dramatic changes in women's fashion. Heavy wool and cotton, the sort of materials that once covered the Victorian woman from head to foot, gave way to light, flimsy synthetics, cut short at the knee and revealing much more of a woman's body. These modern materials, mass-produced in factories, were cheap enough to be replaced each season or each year, according to the whims of a fashion industry that sparkled in the 1920s. New clothes of this type also allowed a much more active lifestyle, whether dancing the Charleston, playing golf and tennis, or riding a bike.

The bicycle itself nearly did away with the earlier convention that young women and men would be chaperoned at all times. By the 1920s the automobile also became ubiquitous, further adding to the privacy enjoyed by young men and women and beginning to earn its sometime reputation as a bedroom on wheels. One final element in the sexual changes of the 1920s involved young men who had been to war and been to France. That double experience added both to their sexual sophistication and their sexual expectations. They might have been to the *Folies Bergere* in Paris or to one of the brothels made available to soldiers at the front. "French postcard" became a synonym for pornographic pictures and "French letter" for condoms. "Ooh la la" became a typical response to all of the above.

The Roaring Twenties could not outlast its decade. Not only did Prohibition end, taking away some of the frisson of a night life in which flappers drank bathtub gin in illegal speakeasies, but the exuberant economy came to a crashing halt, leaving at least half of women as well as men in the United States scrabbling for a bleak existence. Only with the Second World War did women get another chance to come to the aid of their country while also doing well for themselves. Many more women worked in military tasks during World War II than in World War I, a natural progression consistent with modern trends. Many women began to don military uniforms as they joined first the Women's Army Auxiliary Corps (WAAC), created in 1941, and then the Women's Army Corp (WAC), as it became known in 1943. One congressman worried about "who will then do the cooking, the washing, the mending, the humble homey tasks to which every woman has devoted herself?" But the needs of the war effort quickly overcame the anxieties of those politicians whose rural districts might have insulated them from the sort of things to which urban women now devoted themselves.

Some modern women had learned how to fly airplanes. With the outbreak of war, they were recruited to put on a uniform as Women Airforce Service Pilots (WASPs). Some of these women flew heavy bombers produced in Western and Midwestern factories to military bases on the East Coast, in preparation for delivery to Europe. Others became flight instructors, taking on the challenge of teaching men what would have been considered a very masculine task: flying a fighter plane or a bomber. Women who chose to remain in civilian life also gravitated to war work. They became celebrated in the iconic figure of Rosie the Riveter, her hair wrapped in a bandana and her biceps bulging. These women learned to work in heavy industry as effectively as men, producing war materiel and making a good living. The total impact of World War II was much greater than that of World War I. It was a bigger conflict, it lasted longer, and it came after women had already been exposed to significant change in their rights and in their lives, including the right to vote. This war thus produced a generation of women with important new experiences in "men's work" and with high aspirations for their future.

Despite the major impact of World War II, the boost for feminism represented by that war suffered a setback in its aftermath. The same patriotism that pushed women into men's work and justified them in that role, now required that they give their jobs back to the returning male soldiers celebrated as heroes. Postwar women also set about producing the famous Baby Boom, as they welcomed husbands home or attached themselves to freshly-acquired husbands. Furthermore, prosperity in the 1950s nourished the idea of a single breadwinner in the family, with a living wage accessible to the growing middle class and to an increasingly unionized working class. That gave us our Leave-it-to-Beaver image of the 1950s: husbands who go to work, wives who stay at home, a new television in the living room of a suburban home, a green lawn in front, and a Chevy or two in the driveway. This picture was hardly true for all, but it had enough reality so that the progressive changes in women's lives so prominent in the 1920s and during World War II seemed to go in reverse. Gossamer memories leave many of us thinking back to "The Way We Never Were," as Stephanie Coontz has described the 1950s in her book of that name.

The 1960s then exploded in many ways, from the Beatles and the Rolling Stones to Vietnam and antiwar rallies, from Martin Luther King's appeal for non-violent change to Sheriff Bull Connor's German Shepherds, nightsticks, and fire hoses. Betty Friedan launched the modern feminist movement in 1963 with her book, *The Feminine Mystique*. She challenged the idea that women should be pleased with their ostensibly comfortable 1950s version of patriarchy and restricted opportunity. Even before women read Betty Friedan, many of them had begun quite naturally to participate in the changes of the 1960s. They listened to rock and roll. Those who lived in the pampered middle class portion of the population enjoyed their comforts in life, their access to education, their sock hops, their keys to the family car. Some of them became involved in the issues of their day, including the Civil Rights Movement. Just as in the 1840s, women in the 1960s who worked for the rights of African Americans soon saw the need to work for rights of their own.

This interlinked awareness of inequality was part of a much broader pattern, for the Civil Rights Movement inspired many parallel movements among a variety of groups suffering from injustice and discrimination. The 1960s gave birth to Cesar Chavez and the campaign for Latino rights. A student movement for free speech at Berkeley in 1964 quickly became transformed into a campaign for student rights and then into the famous activism of students against the Vietnam War. GLBT agitation for equal rights developed in the 1960s. Public awareness then increased with widespread press attention to the "Stonewall Riots," a violent response in 1969 by gay men and some lesbian women to a New York police raid at the Stonewall Inn in Greenwich Village. In 1970 senior citizens began to advocate for the rights of the elderly in a movement soon dubbed the "Gray Panthers." During the ferment of the 1960s, women too entered perhaps their most active period of equal rights agitation.

All of these movements were based upon the same foundation—a sense of injustice, the ideal that all people should have equal rights, the belief that one's particular group was suffering from stereotyping and discrimination, and the hope that an appeal to the collective conscience of Americans would produce change. Despite the opposition of conservatives at the time, we now acknowledge that those activists who appealed for change in the 1960s were almost always correct in their claims of injustice. We as a society practiced many forms of discrimination, most of them now seen to have been at least inappropriate and in some cases outrageous. Many or most of the changes sought then are now accepted as a matter of course. They polarized society at the time, however. We can see that in the somewhat apoplectic character of Archie Bunker on television. Somewhat like Stephen Colbert today, he played an exaggerated version of right-wing prejudice, giving voice to his grumpy discontent in a manner that made the audience laugh, even as it reflected, perhaps, some of their own problems with changes demanded by women and minorities. Discontent was surely rooted in discomfort with the changes themselves, but it usually also included disapproval of the tactics employed by 1960s activists.

Women at that time borrowed their tactics from the Civil Rights Movement, as did virtually all activist groups. They held consciousness-raising sessions in which women speaking among themselves criticized and challenged the fact that society had taught them to be submissive. They advocated a focus upon women's history, both to celebrate the accomplishments of great women in the past and to identify longstanding and deep-seated patterns of injustice. They organized rallies and demonstrations, hoping to draw media attention to their discontent and gain support for their cause. One of the most famous demonstrations, at the 1968 Miss America Pageant, gave us the expression "bra burning." Even though no bra was burned, due to police concerns about safety on the boardwalk in Atlantic City, this became perhaps the most parodied and pilloried act of 1960s feminists. Women at that protest did *deposit* bras and girdles—along with other "instruments of torture" imposed upon women, such as pots, pans, and copies of *Playboy* magazine—into a large garbage container.

"Women's liberation" became the metaphor that defined the movement, and the convergence of bras and *Playboy* magazines in expression of that metaphor was no coincidence. It voiced the significant claim of modern women in a democratic society that they are more than their bodies. They are more than the eroticized and commercialized portions of their bodies. In the workplace they are more than an object of titillation, a bottom to be pinched, a bosom to be stared at, a potential mistress to be seduced. Both women and blacks struggled in the 1960s and 1970s to be recognized as fully-formed, adult human beings with the capacity to contribute just as much as white men to the betterment of society. Like black Americans, women argued that they had long existed in a world of injustice, suffering denial of their equal rights as citizens. They also argued that this injustice could only be rectified through solidarity among themselves and legal protection under the law.

The first political success of 1960s feminism came with the Equal Pay Act of 1963, banning differential pay on the basis of gender. The next change, with broader implications, came about when Lyndon Johnson pushed the Civil Rights Act of 1964 through Congress. His goal was to ban various forms of discrimination against black Americans. In an odd twist, Howard W. Smith of Virginia added an amendment to include women in its protections. Since Congressman Smith vigorously opposed the Civil Rights Act itself, this amendment has usually been seen as a cynical tactic to try to add more votes to the opposition. If so, it backfired. The House passed the Civil Rights Act and then, after weeks of filibuster, the Senate passed it as well. Suddenly discrimination on the basis of race, sex, religion, national origin, and/or ethnicity was banned in all forms of public accommodation (such as theaters, restaurants, and hotels), in all state and local programs, and in all organizations in receipt of any form of federal funding. The Equal Economic Opportunity Commission (EEOC) grew out of this legislation in 1965 to help enforce it.

"Affirmative action" is another part of this story. The term was first mentioned in an executive order by President Kennedy in 1961, but it grew out of the Civil Rights Act of 1964 and received further impetus in an executive order by President Johnson in 1965. Since that time, the federal government has been on the side of black Americans and women trying to break into types of employment previously considered completely inappropriate for people of "their sort." The very term "affirmative action" recognizes the unavoidable reality that centuries of prejudice and stereotyping—based on both race and gender—weigh heavily in every individual decision to hire a worker, grant a loan, or rent an apartment. If individuals and groups who have suffered a history of discrimination are ever going to overcome the weight of the past, the balancing mechanism has to be adjusted in the short term.

It is working, at least to a degree. Both women and blacks now fill jobs throughout the private and public spheres in numbers that might have been unimaginable to Lyndon Johnson in 1964. Other legislation also had an impact. Title IX of the Civil Rights Act, added in 1972, requires all schools and universities that receive federal funds to provide athletic opportunities for women equal to those available to men. Since Title IX became law, women athletes in basketball, softball, soccer, track and field, and volleyball, among other sports, have learned to swagger on campus much like their male counterparts. They now exhibit team spirit on the field, not just as cheerleaders on the sidelines. They develop the benefits of self-confidence and teamwork, they hone their bodies, and they exhibit a body language known to few women in the 1950s. Women now outnumber men in colleges and universities, earning more undergraduate degrees, with high numbers also in medical schools and law schools.

These changes were unthinkable without the feminists of the 1960s and without government action, such as the addition of women to the Civil Rights Act of 1964. They might even have been unlikely without the threat of bra-burning and other forms of public activism, though that is less certain. What is entirely certain is that women growing up in America in the twenty-first century have a broader set of options and opportunities because of progressive feminists. Conservatives in the 1940s tried to relegate women to the "humble homey tasks to which every woman has devoted herself." Conservatives in the 1960s tried to filibuster the Civil Rights Act of 1964 and other civil rights legislation. But even *conservative* women today—those who run for office, those who run companies—stand on the shoulders of progressive feminists from the past and enjoy their rights as an accepted and welcome feature of the modern world.

Remaining issues

Shared childrearing, shared housework, equal pay for equal work, and perhaps even seven-inch high heels represent issues among American women not yet entirely resolved. The first involves an issue with a biological component, since childbirth and nursing seem now and forever bound to gender. Beyond those two female functions, of course, intelligent and well-meaning couples can learn to share childrearing in a fair and appropriate manner. The same can be said for shared housework. The tasks to be performed within a household bear a heavy residue from our patriarchal past. The evidence suggests that this residue often puts men on the sofa while women complete their second day's work at home. Once again, intelligent and well-meaning couples should be able to learn to count, to measure, and to reach fairness and equity on the issue of shared household tasks.

The problem of equal pay for equal work may carry a more intractable residue of earlier attitudes. Though women began receiving government protection on equal pay in 1963, their actual pay differential has very stubbornly resisted change. Women who work full time today earn 77 cents for every dollar earned by a man. For African-American women the number slips to 62 cents, and for Hispanic women 53 cents. Is that a question of prejudice, as it appears on the surface? Or is it an equitable result of issues that have nothing to do with discrimination? The latter is what Republicans claim when they vote against legislative remediation, as they stubbornly and regularly do. Consider the Paycheck Fairness Act, designed to strengthen the Equal Pay Act of 1963. It passed the House in 2009, received the support of the majority of Americans, and won 58 votes in the Senate in November 2010. Every single Republican Senator opposed this bill, however, and these Republicans used their filibuster tactic to assure that strong majorities in the House, the Senate, and among the public at large were not enough to enact legislation protective of women's rights in the workplace.

A similar stance was taken by conservatives on the Supreme Court in 2007, when they decided 5-4 that Lily Ledbetter could not sue the Goodyear Tire and Rubber Company for wage discrimination. Though she had been paid less than men in comparable work for nearly twenty years, she had not complained to the EEOC within 180 days of being hired. Earlier courts had ruled that the 180-day window opened again with each discriminatory paycheck, but five conservatives on the Supreme Court protected Goodyear by imposing a virtually impossible requirement: Even though Ledbetter had only learned accidentally about the injustice after nearly twenty years of work, the court said her window of opportunity had expired after her first 180 days on the job. This case caused enough outrage so that this time Congress did pass and President Obama signed a "Lily Ledbetter Fair Pay Act" in January 2009. It reestablished the prior principle that each discriminatory paycheck opens a new 180-day window of liability.

The Supreme Court also protected another company against the accusation of discrimination against women. In *Betty Dukes, et al. v. Wal-Mart*, years of discrimination against women in both pay and promotion could easily be shown. However, the court ruled in favor of Wal-Mart, because of the *et al* in the case. Betty Dukes "and others" had brought this as a class action suit, giving them enough leverage and giving attorneys enough incentive to fight the case against a corporation with deep pockets. The court ruled, however, that each woman would have to file her case individually—a virtually impossible task and a decision widely heralded as a major victory for corporations.

Those who oppose women's pay claims in Congress and in the courts, despite the evidence that women earn 77 cents for each dollar earned by a man, usually claim that these pay differentials have nothing to do with gender discrimination. Some say that women earn less because they have less education and experience than men in the same job. Factoring that into the assessment puts women's earnings up to 81 cents on the dollar. Others say that women choose lower paying occupations or are less likely to belong to a union. That can raise the figure to 91 cents. In assessing this line of argument, it should be noted that female secretaries make 83 cents on the dollar earned by male secretaries, though women dominate the occupation as a whole. Such evidence tends to undercut conservative claims about women's "job choices." There is also a question of whether some of the highest paying jobs—on Wall Street, in certain medical practices, in high-profile law firms—involve work climates hostile to women. Is it possible that women are not likely to be hired in the first place in the highest paying occupations, and not as likely to be promoted should they get on the first or middle rung of the ladder? The reality of subtle forms of discrimination is strongly suggested by many studies, as well as by the raw figures of female employment and pay. A study in 2000 noted that when musicians auditioned for an orchestra behind a screen, the percentage of women hired went up. A study in 2008 measured the result of sex change operations. The earnings of men becoming women went down by 32 percent. The earnings of women becoming men went up.

Affirmative action tries to overcome the residue of sexism and racism in employment, with its lingering impact on injustice in our society. Affirmative action is resented by many white men, in some cases quite bitterly and almost always with the charge of "reverse sexism" or "reverse racism." What should an intelligent and fair-minded society do? One cannot "level the playing field" simply by *announcing* that it is level. If every hiring, promotion, and admissions committee is made up of white men, since they are the ones already in place, is it not likely that their natural inclination to replicate themselves might tilt toward white men? Are there not subtle thought processes, judgments, and inclinations which go into hiring and promotion? Is it not even possible that the first women and blacks hired or admitted into a white male world, having learned how to fit in, will be tempted to vote with the dominant white men on hiring and promotion questions? Affirmative action simply suggests that the playing field must be tilted for a period of time in order to make it level. Alternatively, it might never be leveled without that temporary tilt.

White men grew up with advantages, no matter what their background. Deep into the American past there were jobs for which no woman or minority could apply or would ever be considered. That was true also for access to the best educational opportunities. It was even true in terms of which raised hand would be called upon in school, whether white or black, male or female. The same subtle forces apply when a teacher praises or ignores offered opinions. These realities rooted in the past are not hard to locate or difficult to prove. Neither are the real figures that continue to show a differential treatment by gender and race in the way people are employed and paid in American society to this day. The only questions involve how soon and how successfully we as Americans reach a higher level of economic fairness and justice.

The question of seven-inch spiked heels might be harder to adjudicate. Certainly one element of the feminism of the 1960s involved a critique of any sartorial practice that restrained, constricted or damaged a woman's body. Women routinely fainted in the nineteenth century. It was thought to be a feminine quality, a heightened sensibility to emotion, or a natural frailty, but women do not faint like that today. The phenomenon probably involved a shortage of oxygen for women tied too tightly into whalebone corsets. The other complaint 1960s feminists had against women's fashion involved the implication that women are primarily sex objects.

The problems that grow out of the sexual objectification of women are legion. Take body image, for example. Any fat man can look at a woman with an extra five pounds and reject her as too fat, apparently without noticing the irony in his judgment. Eating disorders afflict primarily young women, almost certainly because of societal standards that emphasize female thinness above all. "Young" is another issue here. Male attractiveness can be thought to increase with age (and money, of course), but our society has taught women to despair when they reach thirty, or maybe forty, or maybe fifty. Whatever age is designated as "the new thirty," this age-fixation is surely based on the patriarchal idea that women are above all lithe bodies for sexual gratification.

The sex issue goes far beyond spiked heels or the sexualization of women's bodies rampant in Western culture. As we transition from a patriarchal society with its double standard on sex into a modern society with gender equality, stubborn issues remain. Young women still are the ones who get pregnant, for example. More importantly, there is almost no greater predictor of future economic wellbeing for a woman than her age and circumstance at first pregnancy. Young, single mothers face bleak futures according to all statistical projections, with low pay, high unemployment, and high rates of long-term poverty the norm. That means high rates of poverty for their children too, of course. One of the most problematic trajectories for women in America involves being sexualized at a young age, getting pregnant as a teenager, and entering adulthood with little education, no job, and one or more children. That is also a problem for the nation, since large percentages of these children will grow up in poverty, with limited education, limited healthcare, limited opportunities in life, and limited prospects for getting ahead.

Despite the trajectory I have described and its obvious problems for women, there is a constituency in the United States that vigorously opposes two of the options that can help: sex education and a woman's right to an abortion. It is no coincidence that these two issues converge in one voting group, since each issue has something to do with women's sexuality. Conservative opponents of sex education fear that teenagers, perhaps especially young women, will be more likely to engage in sex if they learn more about it, especially so if they learn about birth control or are given access to condoms. Opposition to sex education, therefore, merges with opposition to the availability of condoms and also with an abstinence-only pledge pushed on young people. Ironically, this approach to sex education, birth control, and abstinence increases rather than decreases teenage pregnancy. That might seem no surprise, since "good" teenagers caught without birth control when their urges overwhelm them are especially vulnerable to conception. But the evidence is more damning than that.

A 2007 report ordered by Congress indicates that abstinence-only sex education has no beneficial impact on sexual behavior. Comprehensive sex education, by contrast, including education on condoms and other forms of contraception, tends to delay sexual activity, reduce the number of partners, increase the use of contraception, and decrease the contracting of STIs (sexually transmitted infections). Obama and a Democratic Congress passed a $190 million program for comprehensive sex education in March 2010, based on this report. However, conservatives pushed to renew an abstinence-only program for an additional five years as well.

Abstinence-only sex education tends to be preferred, of course, in the Bible Belt and in red states in general. Mark Regnerus's book, *Forbidden Fruit: Sex and Religion in the Lives of American Teenagers* (2007) gives a picture of the results. Using government reports as well as interviews with 3400 teenagers aged 13 to 17, he determined that 74% of white evangelical teenagers believe in abstinence. That compares to half of mainline Protestant teenagers and one quarter of Jewish teenagers. However, evangelical teenagers have an earlier sexual "debut," are more sexually active, and use less contraception than mainline Protestants or Jews. This indicates that Bristol Palin's embarrassing pregnancy during the 2008 election was less surprising than it might have seemed at the time.

A report of 2006 indicated that 87% of U.S. high schools taught abstinence. Only 65% taught about the efficacy of condoms, and 39% taught how to use a condom. One way to measure the effectiveness of that sort of education is to look at the number of pregnancies and births among teenage women. By 2005 in the U.S. there were 750,000 teen pregnancies per year, 82% of them unplanned. One quarter of these pregnancies ended in abortions and 59% in live births. This meant a total of 70 births per 1000 American girls aged 15-19. By contrast, Canada had 28 births per 1000 girls of that age and Sweden had 31 births. The level of sexual activity among teenagers in Canada, Sweden, England, France and the United States is similar, though the level of pregnancies and births in those other countries is less than half. Also, American teenagers have shorter relationships, make less use of contraception, and contract much higher rates of STIs. One major variable must be seen as comprehensive sex education, which is much more widely available in advanced nations outside the U.S.

It is also possible to draw comparisons within the United States. A 2006 report by the Guttmacher Institute lists the ten states with the highest rate of births among women 15-19 years old: Mississippi, Texas, Arizona, Arkansas, New Mexico, Georgia, Louisiana, Nevada, Alabama, and Oklahoma in that order. Those regions of our country most likely to vote Republican and most likely to emphasize abstinence have the highest level of pregnancies for teenaged women. Naomi Cahn and June Carbone's book, *Red Families and Blue Families: Legal Polarization and the Creation of Culture* (OUP, 2010), raises the stakes on this comparison. Middle class, blue state families encourage sex education, the use of contraception, and sex as a matter of free choice. Young women raised in that environment have a later sexual "debut," along with much lower rates of teenage pregnancy and STIs. When they go on to finish college, they have an increasing marriage rate and a lowering rate of divorce. If one looks at results instead of rhetoric, the family-friendly portion of America seems clearly to reside in blue states among sexually permissive people. This also happens to produce far fewer of those individuals with whom this discussion began: teen mothers statistically doomed (if not individually doomed) to low levels of education, high levels of unemployment and poverty, and children deprived of a fair start to their lives.

At first glance, the issue of abortion might not seem to be about sex, but about something else. Abortion foes insist on calling the fetus a "baby," they insist on calling abortion "murder," and they claim to have a special reverence for "life." Several things make these claims suspect. First of all, one of the strongest opponents of abortion has always been the Catholic Church. The Catholic Church also opposes birth control. Why? The suspicion arises that Catholic doctrine is simply opposed to sex, especially since various church teachings point in that direction, from St. Paul's "it is better to marry than to burn" to the requirement of a celibate clergy. Rick Santorum, a Catholic, gave further evidence to this idea in his 2012 presidential campaign, with his surprising attack on contraception. In his view, contraception leads to "inappropriate" sex, meaning, of course, sex for pleasure rather than for procreation. In the strict Catholic point of view, no birth control measures should be used to prevent conception and no abortion should be used to terminate a pregnancy. By contrast, secular law in the United States and elsewhere allows contraception. It also distinguishes clearly between a fetus and a baby. The law does not consider an abortion murder, and since 1973 the Supreme Court of the United States recognizes the right of a pregnant woman to choose an abortion.

Evangelical Protestant opponents of abortion do not have the same attitude toward birth control as the Catholic hierarchy, at least not most of them. However, their abstinence-only approach to sex education reflects their conviction that pre-marital and/or promiscuous sex is a serious sin. One might suspect that an unspoken assumption behind the anti-abortion stance found on the evangelical right could be this thought: an unwanted pregnancy is God's way of punishing the sinner. No promiscuous woman should be allowed simply to wash away the evidence of her sin in a doctor's office, possibly even before her shame becomes known to others. So long as abortion remains legal in the United States, these abortion foes skirmish around the edges of the law, placing obstacles in the path of any woman seeking to terminate a pregnancy. They try to shame her into changing her mind and, in a recently-invented tactic, they even propose a vaginal, ultrasound probe of her womb before allowing her to go forward with her choice.

It is worth noting that these same "pro-life" voters often do not revere the lives of those on death row. That is true, even though it is now clear through DNA evidence that a certain number of mistakes occur in capital judgments and some innocent victims certainly have been executed. It is also true that capital punishment continues to reflect a racial divide in the United States, thus making a *prima facie* case for its injustice (see chapter 3). Yet anti-abortion activists regularly support capital punishment for these living, breathing human beings, while they oppose the abortion of a fetus that has never breathed air or taken on the identity of a human being. It is possible to punish a criminal very severely—even including life without parole—without insisting upon execution. Many "pro-life" advocates thus appear not to be pro-life at all. If they have no complaint against capital punishment, they seem simply to be anti-abortion.

These are not easy issues. I am not trying to suggest that having an abortion is a casual matter, something like brushing one's teeth. Human reproduction is important and intensely personal. I am suggesting that abortion might be a best choice in certain circumstances: to protect the life of the mother or to cut short a pregnancy based upon rape, for example. It might also be a preferable option for any woman pregnant against her wishes, at a time when her life and the life of the future child would otherwise be adversely affected. Our legal system has protected this choice since 1973, as have many legal systems elsewhere in the world. Furthermore, the very best way to prevent abortions seems to involve comprehensive sex education and open access to birth control. American abortion rates are higher than in nations where the process is less subject to attack. Those rates could be lowered by accepting human sexuality more realistically, while maintaining the very important right of women to make this choice.

Finally, beliefs imposed by particular versions of the Christian faith—whether Catholic or Protestant—should not be the basis for law in a democratic, pluralist nation. Abortion has become a wedge issue for the Christian right. It represents their effort to stir up voters, apply a litmus test for judges, and work toward overturning Roe v. Wade. Another issue, same-sex marriage, represents a second emotional cause for the Christian right. In this case they want to thwart recent developments toward equal rights for gays and lesbians. In both cases the claims of the Christian right are based on their particular understanding of the Christian faith, an understanding hardly shared by all Christians, much less by those outside the Christian faith. In 1960, when John F. Kennedy ran as a Catholic for the presidency, he praised and supported the separation of church and state in our political system. Rick Santorum, a Catholic from today's Christian right, recently declared that reading Kennedy's speech made him "want to throw up."

What is wrong with this picture? Americans regularly deplore fundamentalist Muslims who believe they should impose Sharia law within the state. Holding up a mirror to that criticism suggests that fundamentalist Christians have no right to impose their religious beliefs on the American legal system. In terms of abortion, individuals who do not approve of it need not have one. The present state of American law and the wisdom of the U.S. Supreme Court thus seem appropriate: each woman should have the right to choose whether abortion is best for her in a given situation. Paying attention to the distinction our language already shows us—a fetus is not a child, abortion is not murder—helps add clarity and reduce emotion. Honoring the separation of church and state leaves specific religious beliefs outside the law, where they belong. Recognizing that a certain group of men, mostly rooted in patriarchal points of view, are among the most vehement opponents of abortion, adds one final reason to acknowledge that this really is an issue involving the rights of women. As with all such issues, the left has always been right. Progressive ideas produce the best as well as the most equitable results.

CHAPTER 3: RACE

Race and gender represent two of the issues by which to see most clearly that the left has always been right. Conservatives today simply accept what conservatives in the past opposed, since a failure to do so would invite universal ridicule and further impugn their credibility. Still, there remain some who dispute the gains of the women's movement. Some groups in the United States today, usually based on religious beliefs, still argue that a woman's only appropriate place is in the home, submitting to the authority of her husband. Even those groups, however, do not try to overturn women's suffrage or a woman's right to participate in the legal system. In terms of race, virtually no one today would argue in public that an African American's place is on the plantation. That point of view has been well and truly buried, recognized as a part of our shameful past. Nonetheless, it is clear that public and private attitudes diverge to a certain extent on race. Some rightwing fringe groups clearly remain entirely racist, and some individuals closer to the center of the spectrum retain racist prejudices they know better than to express in public. But the standard and widespread American point of view today accepts that slavery was wrong and that racism is unacceptable. The left was right on that.

The primary conservative response to the race question today is to claim that we live in a post-racial society, a society in which race no longer matters. Conservatives cite Martin Luther King, Jr., yearning for a time when we will no longer judge people by the color of their skin, and they claim that we are there. Some then call it reverse racism if we continue to pay attention to skin color, insisting that whites are now the main victims. This is where a glance at some numbers and a close look at history are in order.

Our indices of shame

No one likes to feel shame. All of our chants of "we're #1" and the frequent claim of many Americans that the United States is "the greatest nation in the world" nurture national pride and bury any thought of shame. It feels better that way. Also, there exist good reasons for Americans to be proud. The United States is an enormously rich and successful nation. America dominated the twentieth century with economic and military power and remains perched on the top rung of the ladder, even if some of the nervous or prescient think they detect a wobble. America also has been admired, not just envied or feared.

Some of those abroad who use the term "Americanization" see it as an epithet, something to warn against or regret. But many throughout the world aspire to live like Americans and look like Americans. They wear blue jeans and T-shirts. They listen to jazz and to rock and roll. They watch American movies. The world has gone casual, because Americans are casual. In Britain today people have started to call each other by their first names. The collapse of the Soviet Bloc certainly came about at least partly, maybe mostly, because people under communism yearned for the more open American lifestyle and access to consumer goods. That is what Gorbachev had to confront just as much as he had to confront the American force of arms. Furthermore, we Americans have not only been admired for our lifestyle, envied for our wealth, and feared for our military power. We have also been admired for our political ideals. Democracy and free speech in a society based upon freedom, equality, and justice— these are ideals modeled in the United States and either emulated or desired elsewhere.

So what can we Americans do with our many indices of shame? American students compete very badly in math and science. Tested against students in 30 advanced countries in 2006, our fifteen-year-olds placed 17th in science and 24th in math. Our infant mortality rate in 2005 placed us 30th in the world. In 2010 22% of U.S. children lived in poverty, with at least 20% either going hungry or being "food insecure." This is a problem unmatched in Canada or any West European nation, not to mention the fact that those countries all provide some form of universal health care and America does not. These seem like shocking statistics for a nation that considers itself the best in the world.

As for prisons, that is a category where we Americans really have established ourselves as #1. Our rate in 2009 of 743 incarcerated persons per 100,000 people places us far ahead of second place Russia, with its 584 per 100,000. Canada incarcerates only 116 per 100,000 and the European average is about 100. Before 1980, we were not particularly good at this, with only 500,000 prisoners compared to the 2.3 million prisoners in the U.S. now. That meant a rate of only about 200 per 100,000. At approximately 750 prisoners per 100,000 today, we are second in the all-time record books, falling behind only Russia during the pre-World War II horror of Stalin's gulags. He established the apparent record at 800 per 100,000. That hardly seems a feat we would want to surpass or a #1 rating to which we should aspire.

A somewhat similar story involves the American use of capital punishment. This form of punishment used to be common throughout the world, used for every crime from picking pockets to murder or treason. However, execution increasingly came to be considered excessive, even barbaric. First, the range of capital crimes became reduced. Now capital punishment itself is considered unacceptable in virtually every modern, advanced nation except for the United States. No nation may be admitted to the European Union, for example, without first removing any residual death penalty from its legal system. If the use of capital punishment actually deterred capital crimes, that might be a useful argument in the American refusal to give it up. However, despite what some like to think of as the deterrent effect of executions, we Americans murder each other at a pace four times the rate found in England, six times that of Germany, France, or Italy, seven times that of Norway and twelve times that of Japan.

One other set of numbers can catch Americans by surprise: We are not even as rich as many think. Although our national GDP leads the world, our per capita income places us only 18th, behind Norway, Switzerland, Sweden, Denmark, the Netherlands, and Finland, as well as several oil-rich nations and several small tax havens. Some of those nations have very high costs of living, of course. If purchasing power is taken into account, we Americans find ourselves in 7th place according to the IMF and the World Bank, and in 9th place as reported in the CIA *Factbook*. Rich Americans really are very rich. Our unusually high gap between rich and poor has the effect of making us seem a poorer nation on these international charts, despite much impressive wealth. The same can be said about our national place on tables of infant mortality, teen scores in math and science, or rates of incarceration.

Our indices of shame do not really illuminate the lives of rich Americans, or even middle class Americans. Rather, they point toward gross inequalities and gaps in the American experience. If one analyzes these numbers by race, they highlight even more shameful discrepancies. Every school district in the nation is trying to raise the test scores of African-American children, Hispanic children, and American Indian children, because their average test scores are markedly low. Every prison and jail in the United States is filled disproportionately with African Americans, so that approximately one of every three black men is statistically destined for prison in our country. The ratio of people living in poverty is also weighted toward people of color. In 2011 when the American unemployment rate was hovering at 9%, the percentage of blacks unemployed was more than 15% and the percentage of young black males unemployed was well over 30%.

There are those who will look at every one of these indices and blame the aggregate results on individual mistakes and bad choices. There are also those, the most racist among us, who will accept the aggregate nature of the results and simply see black Americans as less intelligent, less motivated, less hardworking, and less disciplined than whites. That is a comforting thought to a racist, since it suggests that prejudice and discrimination are not the source of the problem. The racist rationalization is that our problems are not the fault of white Americans, but the fault of black Americans. Yet the comfort to be gained from that idea is fragile at best, as a closer look at some of our indices of shame makes clear.

Consider some statistics on drug use and drug incarceration. In 2009 illicit drug use by whites was assessed at 8.2% and by blacks at 10.1%. Yet in 2006, drug prisoners were 44% black and 28% white. Naturally, blacks who represent only 13% of the U.S population form a much smaller pool, so that the per capita rate of incarceration for black drug crime is about 10 times higher than for whites. That obviously bears no relation to actual rates of illicit drug use by the two groups. Similar statistics can be found for incarceration in general. In 2007, 40% of incarcerated males were black and 33% white. The rate of incarceration that year was 4,618 per 100,000 for black men and 773 per 100,000 for white men. That is a differential of about 6 to 1. A Stanford study in 2009 observed such statistics and came to the obvious conclusion: In the war on drugs—the main factor increasing the number of incarcerated Americans from 500,000 before 1980 to 2.3 million today—black Americans are disproportionately targeted by police, by prosecuting attorneys, and by juries.

The same color-coded tendency holds true in the statistics on capital crimes and capital punishment. If we look at figures from 1976 (when capital punishment became legal again, after a brief hiatus) to the year 2011, prisoners executed in the United States were 35% black (a total of 440 executions), 7% Hispanic (95 executions), and 56% white (714 executions). Considering the much larger white population in the U.S., that already suggests disproportion. Disproportionate justice is confirmed if we look at the imposition of the death penalty in relation to the race of the victims of capital crimes. A study in North Carolina in the 1990s determined that a death penalty was 3.5 times more likely if the victim had been white. If we look back nationally to 1976, we find only 17 executions of whites convicted of murdering a black victim, and 254 executions of blacks convicted of murdering a white victim. Finally, the percentages of blacks and Latinos on death row today equal 42% and 12% respectively, with whites at only 44%. As is known from several recent cases, DNA and other forms of evidence have shown that at least some people on death row have been wrongly convicted, almost certainly with racial stereotypes playing at least a partial role.

The International Convention on the Elimination of all Forms of Racial Discrimination (ICERD), a convention ratified by the United States along with many other nations, states categorically that a determination of racial discrimination does not require malign intent. Disparate results measured by race are sufficient to prove that racism exists. When the U.S. ratified this convention, we did so with various reservations and declarations designed to ensure that it not be used against us. American statistics on race and crime, however, along with our statistics on poverty, education, and employment all suggest that systemic racism continues to exist in the United States. These statistics should make us extremely skeptical of any claim that we Americans live in a post-racial or non-racist society. That claim does not pass the sniff test. Those who think otherwise simply do not place their nose near the evidence and take that sniff. Furthermore, alongside the many statistical indicators of racial injustice, we also have another form of evidence: nearly four centuries of North American history.

New World slavery and American attitudes toward race

It is comforting for white Americans to think that slavery once existed throughout the world and that racism has been ubiquitous in all cultures. Neither is quite true. At the very least, the implications of that comforting idea are quite misleading. All serious history of slavery acknowledges that something very important changed about four hundred years ago, when capitalist production and race-based slavery combined in the New World. Previous examples of slavery had involved Greeks enslaving their neighbors, Romans enslaving their neighbors, or Africans enslaving their neighbors. Slaves were often those unlucky enough to have been captured in war or poor enough to have sold themselves into slavery. They were not thought to be especially suited for slavery based upon their skin color, which was usually the same as their owner, nor were their children, grandchildren, and great-grandchildren expected to be slaves. Furthermore, slaves were primarily put to work within the household, assisting at tasks that might include preparing food, washing the dishes, or caring for children. In other words, they tended to be members of the household living within the household, in some cases almost like another member of the family. Most early forms of slavery did not involve mass production of a marketable commodity in a process designed to create wealth for the slave owner.

New World circumstances created a very different form of slavery and this new form intensified its brutality and multiplied its ill effects in two crucial ways. The first difference was economic. When Europeans reached the Americas, it was at an early stage of modern capitalism. The ability to produce a commodity like tobacco, rice, indigo, sugar, or cotton had almost nothing to do with what one personally wanted to smoke, eat, drink, or wear. Those early New World entrepreneurs were not producing to consume, but rather to sell. If they could sell sugar, tobacco or cotton abroad, they could then buy their necessities and/or luxuries with cash. They could dress in the latest European fashions, rather than homespun, wear silk rather than cotton. If they could expand their operation enough, they could afford luxuries of every sort.

Land was cheap and easy to acquire in seventeenth-century America, once the Indians were pushed aside. Labor was the sticking point. No single individual or family household could raise enough of a commodity to grow rich, no matter how much land they could acquire. With the first importation of slaves, the second half of the equation fell into place. Land plus labor equaled wealth, and the leverage was fantastic. Wealth could expand exponentially if one could add dozens or hundreds of slaves to hundreds or thousands of fertile acres. The Spanish in Central and South America and the Portuguese in Brazil were the first to invent this system, importing millions of Africans to the New World. Then English sugar planters in the Caribbean followed suit. Beginning in 1619, English colonists in Virginia imported their first African workers.

This change in the nature of slaves' work dramatically worsened the life of slaves. They became a dehumanized cog in an economic machine, valuable insofar as they could produce more wealth than their cost in food and shelter. Slave owners had a strong incentive to maximize production through long hours, harsh discipline, and year-round tasks. They had very little incentive to make life pleasant, except perhaps to stave off open rebellion. Furthermore, staving off rebellion might be accomplished more effectively with harsh punishment than with humane treatment. They were not modern liberals, with soft notions about how to change human behavior. Instead, they turned quickly to whipping, branding, maiming, or even occasionally to executing a slave. Though the execution cost them a valuable commodity, it could set an example for others.

Field hands producing cash crops labored long hours in harsh conditions. On large plantations they lived in slave quarters far removed from their owner. They were likely to work under the whip of an overseer, rather than under the eye of their owner, which lessened the chance that an owner might feel the tug of common humanity. Some house slaves may have benefited from the normal human bonds that develop within a household, though even they were subject to rape, family separation, and the reality that they were owned as property. Field hands were the most likely to be dehumanized within this system, viewed more as machines or beasts of burden than fellow human beings.

Race provided the second iniquitous element in New World slavery, alongside the impact of a market economy. Never before had one race been set outside the human family and identified as an appropriate source of slave labor. Never before had millions of people been captured and transported from one continent to another, in the most inhumane and miserable circumstances, to meet the labor needs of another group of people. Approximately twenty million Africans were captured and sold to slave traders from the sixteenth through the nineteenth century. This process did not involve Europeans venturing into the interior of Africa. Rather, they set up trading centers along the coast and relied upon tribal differences within Africa and the lure of financial gain to fill the cages they built. When sufficient numbers were secured, they crowded the captured Africans into boats, either tightly or loosely packed, depending on how individual slave merchants assessed the issue of "wastage" on the voyage. A tightly packed ship meant more slaves to sell, but also a higher rate of "loss" during the voyage, due to the increasingly inhospitable conditions onboard. It is estimated that some ten million captured Africans died between the time of their capture and the time of their purchase at a slave auction in the New World.

For Europeans in the Americas desiring cheap labor, African slaves were not the first or only option. Native peoples were enslaved, for example, a practice that provides an early example of racial stereotyping as a way to soothe the conscience of Euro-American entrepreneurs. In his book, *The Invasion of America: Indians, Colonialism, and the Cant of Conquest* (1976), Francis Jennings describes many ways in which racial stigma conveniently made savages out of the Indians. That negative term, "savage," minimized the quite large native population base and the quite varied lifestyle. It underplayed the role of farming and agriculture among Indians and emphasized the threat of warrior violence. It justified the European conquest of America as the "discovery" of an essentially "un-peopled wilderness," roamed but not really inhabited by those "few" savages. There were enough native peoples to provide a potential source of slave labor, of course, but they did not prove very useful. Given their vulnerability to European diseases, they died off quickly. They also were likely to escape, because they knew the landscape and could find friendly assistance nearby.

White indentured servitude provided another source of labor, one that dominated English North America during the seventeenth century. Indentured servants could earn passage to the New World by signing a labor contract for up to seven years. One problem was that these indentured servants could not be kept beyond their contracted term of service, nor could their children and grandchildren be added to the pool of coerced and unpaid labor. Another problem involved their white skin. If they were to run away, it was not easy to track them down or identify them in Boston or some other city, since they could blend into the rest of the population. It was also harder psychologically to dehumanize white-skinned indentured servants, since they came from the same Christian culture and often spoke the same language as their masters.

African slaves mitigated these difficulties in various ways. Rooted for millennia in the Old World, the interconnected continents of Europe, Asia, and Africa, they were more resistant to European germs than were Indians. Thus they not only could survive in the New World, they could even reproduce and prosper physically, resulting in a strong and growing labor force. Their distinctive skin color made it very difficult for them to run away and relatively easy to recapture if they did. In slaveholding regions, any black person could be presumed a slave and apprehended, so that travel passes for slaves and official papers carried by free blacks became necessities. Race was even more important on a psychological level. It must have been difficult for anyone to participate in the implementation of slavery—witnessing first hand the horror of slave auctions, the agony of families being separated, the brutality of whippings and other punishments employed to keep slaves in check. How could one not feel some rising up of human compassion or an overwhelming sense of guilt? Racial stereotyping, in other words *racism*, conveniently provided the anesthetic.

Did New World Americans invent racism? That might be a stretch. Ethnic and tribal differences have caused animosity and produced trouble throughout history. However, there is no other time or place in which racial stereotyping proved as useful as it did in New World slavery. There is no other example of an entire continent being thought the natural source of human slaves, and no other instance of twenty million people being captured in an attempt to transport them five thousand miles for the purpose of producing wealth for others. Slaves could more easily be seen as "other," even as less than human, when all slaves shared a skin color. Even better, all African slaves could be traced to a continent little known to Europeans and much despised as dark, forbidding, and, perhaps most importantly, non-Christian.

Many excuses were invented to justify slavery. For example, it was often said that African slaves were really lucky to have been brought to a rich, Christian country, where they could benefit from material advantages in the here and now and have a chance to go to heaven in the hereafter. The rightwing political figure, Patrick Buchanan, recently revived this argument on his website with his controversial claim that "America has been the best country on earth for black folks." Here they were "introduced to Christian salvation and reached the greatest levels of freedom and prosperity blacks have ever known." (The same website suggests Buchanan's relaxed assessment of Adolf Hitler and the Holocaust in the title of one of his books, *Churchill, Hitler, and the Unnecessary War: How Britain Lost its Empire and the West Lost the World*.)

Most now see the claim that Africans were lucky to be brought to America as slaves as both self-serving and casually dismissive of the harshness experienced by those Africans. They were captured, transported, sold, brutally worked, and then, even after the end of slavery, treated to more than a century of harsh racism and legal repression. These claims about "lucky" slaves also tend to be ignorant of African history and culture. While Europe was mired in the Dark Ages, a time when reading and writing practically disappeared, Africans had universities at places like Timbuktu. Muslims in North Africa preserved and studied Aristotle at a time when he had been entirely lost to Europe. Africans had developed the political skill to organize large political entities, like the Kingdom of Ghana and the Kingdom of Mali. Alex Haley studied his own family and produced *Roots*, both as a book and as a television miniseries. He describes his forebear, Kunta Kinté, as a child who studied the Koran and had been taught to read and write. Auctioneers in America, however, were likely to describe newly arrived slaves as "monkeys" fresh out of the trees in African jungles. The utility of that willful ignorance is obvious.

The best excuse of all to justify slavery, and one that developed routinely in North America, was that God created black people specifically to serve as slaves to whites. All of the elements in what became known as the "Sambo thesis" match the sort of characteristics most suitable to someone forced to be a slave. Blacks were thought to be childlike, thus in need of whites to guide and teach them. Blacks were thought to be happy-spirited, thus untroubled by the sort of lifelong drudgery that would undo a white, given the white person's natural aspirations for a higher mode of life. Blacks' apparent propensity for singing and dancing was thought to be adequate proof of their childlike, happy nature. Of course, it is now known that much of the singing involved spirituals like "Go down Moses," based upon stories of Israelites yearning to be free. Blacks were seen as strong, thus capable of the work they were required to do, but also clumsy, likely to break tools. Historians now give them proper credit and suspect that many slaves broke their tools in order to get some slack time before that tool could be replaced. The result was that hoes soon had enormously thick and heavy handles in an attempt to hinder the breakage.

The "Sambo thesis" includes "yes massa" black people—bowing and shuffling, head down, the picture of deference. This image was so strong it was depicted in Hollywood eight decades after the end of slavery, with the very successful dancer, Bill "Bojangles" Robinson, playing the black servant to Shirley Temple's preternaturally wise and sensible little girl. In one film Bill Robinson is so childlike and ignorant that he sees a billowing white sheet and goes all fluttery, thinking it a ghost. Shirley Temple, the little girl, says, "Don't be silly. There aren't any ghosts." On the athletic field, a parallel can be found in the long-delayed advent of black quarterbacks in American football. Until relatively recently, coaches and football executives doubted the ability of black quarterbacks to master the intellectual requirements of the position and/or they doubted the willingness of other players to accept black leadership. This is a prejudice that now seems ludicrous. However, it reflects the essential story in the view white America invented about black people, that they are physically useful, but not mentally capable, all brawn and no brain—perfect for slavery, in fact, just as God intended.

If one analyzes these stereotypes, the first thing to be noted is that they almost perfectly match the stereotypes maintained by the worst American racists today. One also can detect certain ways in which slaves would likely have behaved in order to marginally improve their existence. Singing songs to create some pleasure in their lives, especially if the songs are about freedom, and breaking tools to gain some down time seem like good strategies. Showing deference was also useful, since not showing deference would almost certainly lead to a whipping and permanent scars across one's back. At least into the 1950s in the American South, black people who did not show deference, black people who did not look at the ground when talking to whites, especially to white women, were likely to be lynched!

Brutal death is what happened to Emmett Till, a black fourteen-year-old from Chicago visiting relatives in Mississippi in the summer of 1955. Not familiar with southern ways and dared by friends to talk to the white woman in a small store, he cheekily said "Bye baby" as he walked out the door. Her husband and brother-in-law kidnapped Emmett Till, gouged out an eye, caved in one side of his skull, put a bullet in his brain, and dumped his corpse into a river. When put on trial for murder, their defense attorney appealed to the all-white, all-male jury not to make their "fathers turn over in their graves." No white in Mississippi had ever been convicted for murdering a black. These jurors lived up to their southern tradition, letting the murderers go free. Emmett Till's tragic mistake was not to know the level of deference required of blacks in the aftermath of slavery in the American South. To see deference or other learned and necessary behaviors under slavery as somehow indicative of black people's basic nature is a convenience to the racist, but easily dissected by any rational person. Alex Haley's *Roots*, the miniseries from 1977, shows black people behaving like deferential, contented children among whites, and like angry, strong, intelligent adults among themselves in their slave quarters. That is almost certainly much closer to the truth.

Patrick Buchanan and others want to argue that Africans were lucky to be brought to America as slaves. Those in the South who fly the Confederate flag want to argue that they are simply endorsing Southern culture, not a prejudice against blacks. Those conservatives who scream "reverse racism" in their attacks on affirmative action or other progressive developments emerging from the Civil Rights Movement want to claim that their stance is not based upon racial prejudice. Republican voters in the American South do not acknowledge that they are influenced by a racist past in their present political preferences. They fail to keep in mind the story of Emmett Till. They fail to acknowledge how recently courts in the American South made a mockery of justice across racial lines. They fail to realize how deeply American attitudes about race are rooted in just those arguments and claims once most useful to quiet the conscience of the slaveholder, the sort of arguments and claims still most likely to be a staple in the arsenal of racists today.

Any objective look at New World slavery seems certain to show that whites in the Western Hemisphere invented the worst form of slavery in human history—as extreme as that might sound. It also suggests that white Americans invented or at least intensified the human tendency toward race-based prejudice. The story of Emmett Till in 1955 is a grim reminder of that prejudice. One can also note that Europeans (after the fall of Rome) did not practice slavery. No system of slavery developed in Germany, France or England. No large population of enslaved Africans entered the demography of those nations. When black American GIs got to England and France during World War I, and on to Germany during and after World War II, they were surprised to be treated like human beings. That helps account for a large number of black American soldiers who remained in France after 1918. Black American culture developed a vibrant presence in Paris of the 1920s, with jazz clubs and Josephine Baker. Writers of the Harlem Renaissance spent time in Paris, including Langston Hughes. Both Richard Wright and James Baldwin moved to Paris after World War II.

It is not that Europeans exhibited no prejudice or held no negative stereotypes about people of color. Germans, after all, took racism to new heights in the Nazi era. Also, racism and prejudice have increased in Western Europe since the 1960s, when migrations from former colonies began to change demographics in places like England and France. But African Americans who reached Europe in the eighteenth, nineteenth or twentieth century were most likely to find it a remarkably welcoming place in comparison to what they experienced at home. Another example of the difference between European and American attitudes can be seen in race riots in England during World War II. These did not involve English mistreatment of black GIs. They involved racial animosities within the segregated American forces that often broke out into violence. As a result, the American military tried to get the English to establish a color bar in their pubs and other establishments, something previously unknown in their culture. One riot between white and black Americans in Bristol was so fierce that it had to be put down by a force of 300 troops. Black Americans fought for the United States during both of the World Wars, but it was only after World War II that Harry Truman began insisting on integration within our armed forces, and the path toward fair and just treatment began.

There is one last, disconcerting element in the history of New World racism. Scholars in the 1940s and 1950s began to notice that the color bar in the United States remained much more rigid than in Central and South America. By mid-century, for example, marriage between whites and blacks was forbidden in 29 of the 48 American states, though it was legal and common in former Spanish colonies and in Portuguese-influenced Brazil. Frank Tannenbaum of Columbia University published a book in 1947, *Slave and Citizen*, which compared experiences in the United States with Latin America. He emphasized culture, arguing that the greater freedom in England's colonies allowed local slave owners greater latitude. They used it, ironically, to develop a harsher regimen for their slaves. Spain and Portugal were more authoritarian, both in their centralized ideas of government and in the hierarchy of the Catholic Church. When the king of Spain or the pope in Rome demanded that slaves be treated with some restraint, it might have had an impact. Furthermore, these nations used Roman Law, which included protections for slaves, whereas English Common Law developed when no slaves existed in England. Thus slaves in North America fell into the one category left to them under English Common Law, that of property. You can mistreat your cow or horse, even if it might seem counterproductive. The same held true for slaves.

Later historians questioned some of the cultural assumptions proposed by Tannenbaum. For one thing, Spanish and Portuguese slave owners were hardly benign. When price and availability allowed, for example, they often worked slaves to death and purchased new ones, rather than pay for a higher level of care. Instead of looking at culture, more historians today look to economic and demographic explanations in trying to make sense of differential treatment. For example, plenty of whites arrived in the English colonies to fill mid-range jobs, such as artisan, overseer, or militiaman. By necessity, these jobs involved more independence than manual labor in a field gang, and these jobs also receive more respect. A shortage of Spanish and Portuguese men in Central and South America required that whites there turn to a free black workforce to perform these necessary tasks, which broke down the color-based assumption that blacks were not smart enough to learn higher-level skills.

Gender balance also differed in the two regions. Spanish and Portuguese settlers were primarily male. If they were to have wives and children, some of those wives would have to be black and the resulting children mulatto. In that case, white fathers needed to smudge the color line in order to bequeath their power and wealth to their own children. In North American colonies by contrast, English settlement soon included substantial numbers of women as well as men. Some of those white men did have sex with black women. However, since they also had white wives, they had a very strong incentive to bequeath their power and wealth to their legal, white children, and completely to deny their paternity in the case of mulattos. That is almost certainly the origin of the strange North American custom by which a person with any trace of black ancestry is considered black, no matter what the ratio of white blood in his or her veins. Such an attitude seems almost the definition of a rigid color bar.

Political implications of the American legacy of race

Since the American Civil Rights Movement, attitudes on race have changed dramatically. However, many of today's adults have absorbed these changes on the fly, modifying the overtly racist assumptions of their youth with the politically correct notions on race now widely accepted. This can result, of course, in a more veiled and sublimated version of racism. Consider an incident involving Mike Huckabee before he decided not to run for president in 2012. He had the misfortune to suggest on a radio program that President Obama did not learn to know America as "the rest of us" did, because he spent his childhood in Kenya. This comment was unfortunate first of all since it was flat wrong. Obama did not even visit Kenya until he was an adult. It was also unfortunate, because it allows us to ask where Mike Huckabee grew up. Born in Arkansas in 1955, he experienced the 1950s and 1960s in a state where conservative policies held sway and black people knew "their place." Blacks in Arkansas at that time had to accept whites-only schools, restaurants, hotels, benches, and drinking fountains. They learned to show deference if they did not want to suffer a cross burned in their front yard or a lynching. Is that the 1950s America valued by conservatives? Is that the sort of nostalgic world that nurtured "real Americans," the best Americans? Outcomes were not automatic. Bill Clinton also grew up in Arkansas. But to grow up white in mid-century Arkansas and then emerge a Republican means almost certainly that one at least mingles with racists, some covert and some probably overt.

Barack Obama, born in 1961 in Hawaii, did not grow up in Mike Huckabee's American South. He not only was raised in the rainbow state of Hawaii, he even spent some time living with his white mother while she did development work in Indonesia. As an adult, Obama turned his tremendous intelligence, hard work, and ambition—characteristics that completely defy white racist stereotypes—into a Harvard education, a career in law, and a political trajectory that brought him to the White House. What Huckabee seems not to have sensed is that Barack Obama's open, multiracial Hawaii of the 1960s mirrors the makeup and climate of today's America. The segregationist, racist Arkansas of the 1950s does not.

An earlier generation of southern white politicians gives us a more graphic picture of the influences that led to the composition and policies of today's Republican Party. Strom Thurmond, born in 1902, worked his way up in South Carolina politics until he won the governorship in 1946. He ran as a Democrat. That was the only party in South Carolina with any chance for success, ever since Abraham Lincoln, as a Republican, ordered troops to fire on Fort Sumter and started the Civil War. (There was an exception during post-Civil War Reconstruction, when blacks briefly were allowed to vote and Republicans were the progressive party). In 1948 Thurmond entered national politics as the third-party presidential nominee of the States' Rights Democratic Party. These "Dixiecrats," as they became known, represent the first strong indication that white southern Democrats increasingly held misgivings about their national party and its progressive tendencies. The last straw for Thurmond and his friends occurred when Harry Truman announced the racial integration of American military forces in 1948. Part of Thurmond's campaign that year included this straightforward comment: "I wanna tell you, ladies and gentlemen, that there's not enough troops in the army to force the Southern people to break down segregation and admit the nigger race into our theaters, into our swimming pools, into our homes, and into our churches."

Though Thurmond and these breakaway Democrats could not thwart Truman's reelection in 1948, South Carolina and three other southern states cast their electoral votes for his Dixiecrat ticket. In 1954 Thurmond ran as a Democrat and got elected to the Senate. He then served as a Democratic member of the Senate for ten years, before casting his support to Barry Goldwater in the presidential election of 1964 and switching officially to the Republican Party himself. Goldwater had voted against Lyndon Johnson's Civil Rights Act of 1964. This endeared him to Thurmond, who opposed civil rights and advocated for states' rights throughout his career. The two issues went together. If states were allowed the freedom to set their own policies, no civil rights for black residents would be allowed to slip across South Carolina's borders. In opposition to a proposed Civil Rights Act in 1957, the freshman Senator Thurmond indicated his priorities and put himself in the record books. He filibustered against that legislation for twenty-four hours and eighteen minutes, the longest individual filibuster in Senate history. As a result, the Civil Rights Act did not pass until Lyndon Johnson pushed it through in 1964.

When Thurmond made his switch to the Republican Party in 1964, he managed to bring South Carolina with him. That made Goldwater the first Republican to win South Carolina since Reconstruction, and South Carolina has been reliably Republican ever since. Thurmond himself served eight full terms and set a record for the oldest sitting Senator in history when he turned 100 in 2002. That year he finally chose not to run for reelection, and he died in June 2003. Throughout his final 38 years, Thurmond continuously pushed the Republican Party to the right. He delivered an increasingly solid Republican South, always with pressure on national Republicans to stop courting moderate to liberal voters with Republicans like Nelson Rockefeller of New York, Mark Hatfield of Oregon, or Charles Percy of Illinois. Richard Nixon cooperated in 1968 by selecting Spiro Agnew as his running mate, a safely conservative if somewhat criminal governor of Maryland, rather than a moderate with more appeal in the North.

Jesse Helms, a younger colleague of Strom Thurmond, represents a similar trajectory. Born in 1921, his first foray into North Carolina politics came while working on publicity for Willis Smith in the Democratic senatorial primary of 1950. Together they attacked a respected, liberal Democrat, Frank Porter Graham, for "mingling the races." They also produced a flier with the demagogic message, "Wake up, white people." This emphasis on anti-black politics in North Carolina in the 1950s, when only white people were allowed to vote, won Smith the nomination and the election. Helms followed him to Washington as his administrative assistant. In 1960 Helms worked for Beverly Lake in the governor's race. Lake's main campaign platform was to resist the integration of North Carolina schools as demanded by the U. S. Supreme Court. Though Lake lost that election to a moderate, Terry Sanford, Helms continued throughout the 1960s to burnish his credentials as an anti-integration conservative, a believer in states' rights and an opponent of federal intervention. He suggested that a wall be built around the University of North Carolina at Chapel Hill, that "university of Niggers and Communists," so that the rest of the state would not be tainted by liberal ideas.

By 1972 Jesse Helms had not changed his politics—he still opposed integration, he opposed abortion, he backed states' rights against federal intervention, and he backed prayer in public schools. But Helms did change parties, switching from the Democratic Party that had once dominated the South into the Republican Party of Nixon's "southern strategy." Helms won a Senate seat that year. For the next 30 years—five full terms—he served as one of the most conservative senators in the Republican caucus. His was an aggressive voice, unashamedly out of step with the Senate and the nation as a whole, filibustering for his causes, blocking federal appointments by Democratic and Republican presidents alike, and making trouble even for Ronald Reagan, when Reagan took his occasional step toward pragmatic centrism.

Both Thurmond and Helms seemed extremely rightwing in the Republican Party of the 1970s, when pragmatic moderates still held an important place in the party. Both supported the conservative shift led by Reagan in the 1980s, but stood to his right. Now, however, the legacy of Thurmond and Helms, an aggressive rightwing agenda without compromise, dominates the Republican Party. That could be seen when Tea Party Republicans humiliated their own Speaker of the House, John Boehner, and nearly shut down the nation in August 2011, rather than approve a routine and necessary extension of the national debt limit. Standard & Poor's bond rating agency noticed and reduced the United States' perfect AAA debt rating for the first time in history. It was in the spirit of Strom Thurmond and Jesse Helms when Goerge W. Bush won the crucial South Carolina primary against John McCain in 2000, using a nasty (and untruthful) whisper campaign that McCain had fathered a black child. It is due to the constituency of Strom Thurmond and Jesse Helms that Republican candidates for the presidency in 2012 have had to flip-flop on many issues in order to pretend to believe in the most rabidly rightwing ideas. All eight candidates, for example, vowed that they never would have accepted the debt limit compromise that saved the nation from bankruptcy in August 2011. And Newt Gingrich won the South Carolina Republican primary in 2012 by calling Barack Obama, our first black president, the nation's "greatest food stamp president," a low and dishonest tactic that virtually all commentators described as a racist appeal to anti-black voters.

Today's Republican Party has deep roots in the states' rights, anti-integration, and anti-black politics of Strom Thurmond and Jesse Helms. It also has its most solid voting bloc among the Thurmond and Helms base, white voters in the South. In fact, without that support in the former Confederacy, the Republican Party of today would have no chance at all of controlling the House or the Senate and no chance of winning the Presidency. The "solid South" is their linchpin, giving them a block of Senate and House seats and presidential electoral votes on which their hopes for a majority always depend.

Does that mean that today's Republican Party shares the racism by which Thurmond and Helms began their political careers? All of today's conservative heirs of Strom Thurmond and Jesse Helms publicly accept the idea that blacks should have equal rights, the sort of changes they fought against during the Civil Rights Movement. Conservatives today are forced to admit, at least implicitly, that conservatives then were wrong and progressives were right. Strom Thurmond and Jesse Helms even made an effort by the 1970s to add a black person or two to their staffs. No one with any commitment to American democracy and the ideas of equality and justice can honestly oppose today's acceptance of equal rights for African Americans, and no one with hopes for political influence in today's America could advocate otherwise. But it is much harder for many conservatives to look deep within and find a multiracial heart. They walk this tightrope both personally and politically, as they seek the support of their natural base.

One hidden detail in Strom Thurmond's biography is worth noting here. He fathered a mixed-race child when he was 22 and his parents' black maid was 16. But that sort of racial mixing had nothing to do with the ideal of racial integration and placed no restraint upon his rabidly anti-integrationist political stance. This part of his life was closer to the tradition dating back to the plantation, when young white men could expect to have sex with black women in subservient positions. Thurmond acknowledged his first wife, who died young. He acknowledged his second wife, whom he married at the age of 66 when she was 23. Both wives came to his attention as winners of the Miss South Carolina beauty pageant. He acknowledged his four white children produced in later years with his second wife. He nurtured his reputation throughout 48 years in the Senate as an incorrigible flirt. Thurmond actually gave some secret financial support to his mixed-race daughter, Essie Mae Washington-Williams, but he kept his youthful liaison completely secret. News of this, which might have stopped his political career in it tracks, came out only after his death.

Strom Thurmond and Jesse Helms represent the first generation of southern, white Republicans, but the deep-seated ideas that supported their political careers have not entirely disappeared. It is this instinctive reaction to questions of race that most likely explains Mike Huckabee's mistake about President Obama and Kenya. It is almost certainly the reason that the "birther" movement could linger for several years, with its implication that Obama could not be a real American, and with very few Republicans willing to put a stake into the heart of that bizarre theory. It probably played a role when Congressman Joe Wilson from South Carolina broke decorum and yelled out "you lie" while Obama spoke to a joint session of Congress in 2009.

The sinews of our past retain a hold on our body politic. Every American over sixty today was born into a United States where racist jokes were common, where blacks could not play sports at any university in the South, where blacks almost never appeared on television, and where thoroughgoing apartheid was implemented throughout a large portion of our country. Black athletes did not play in the NFL or the NBA, and had just begun to follow Jackie Robinson's hard-earned path into major league baseball. Black entertainers could not stay at white hotels or eat in white restaurants in the South.

Every American under forty today, by contrast, grew up in an America were Michael Jordan played basketball at the University of North Carolina and then became the sort of icon whose poster might grace the walls of any young athlete's bedroom anywhere in the United States, regardless of their race. Bill Cosby's portrayal of a kind, wise, and witty father began to transform television, and Colin Powell proved that black Americans can rise to the top in our military. Laws against interracial marriage have long since been banished and the mixing of races socially has become common for many Americans. More interracial marriages and more interracial children are now leading us away from instinctive and deep-seated racism. These are fantastic developments. They might even remove racism from American society over time. But there remain far too many Americans whose gut instincts were formed in our racist past for that racist past to have disappeared. It has been covered over. It peeks out from under the covers. And its defenders, supporters, and natural constituents are to be found on the right.

Lessons?

We Americans can and should celebrate the Civil Rights Movement of the 1960s as one of the great accomplishments in American history. We can recognize that certain remarkable black leaders, individuals such as Martin Luther King, Jr., have brought us—sometimes kicking and screaming—into a much better world. We all accept these changes now. But many of us refuse to accept that there is a connection between our shameful past and our current indices of shame, between the outrageous behavior by which Americans perpetrated the institution of slavery and the fact that black Americans today are far more likely than whites to be undereducated, unemployed, or in jail. The Patrick Buchanans of this world argue that we have already done enough to end racism, that we can put the injustice of slavery and segregation in our rearview mirror. They point to the many government policies since the 1960s and speak begrudgingly about the money spent. They suggest that whites are now the victims, and argue that today there is no appropriate place for "white guilt" or policies based upon it.

Where does that place an intelligent observer, a humane and caring voter? There are, of course, many reasons to end racism and overcome its legacy besides the humane reasons of fairness, equality and justice. Education and job-creation are almost certainly better for our nation than having to pay for social dysfunction. Keeping people out of jail is cheaper than keeping people in jail. Solving the twin problems for African Americans and other minorities of low performance results in school and high unemployment figures in the workplace has to be good for our nation simply in economic terms. If we add what this could do for our sense of ourselves as a fair and just people—not to mention the improvement in our international reputation, where critics now can take note of our hypocrisy—these outcomes would be even better. Can we justify, fund, and perpetuate the programs that conservatives disparage? Can we develop intelligent programs, so that in a generation or two the present disparities will diminish, so that the inherent cost of being born black in America will disappear?

The most important question we can ask about our indices of shame is this: Do they have anything to do with our racist past? Is it merely a coincidence that black Americans as a group struggle in today's America? One problem with the conservative response—blaming the statistics on black people, on black culture, on black choices—is that these responses so completely resemble the racist stereotypes we whites invented in this country to justify slavery and segregation. More than other nations or cultures, white Americans learned to rely on disparagement of black people in order to justify a system of exploitation virtually unique in world history. If that claim seems too strong, then consider the American system of exploitation merely *one* of the most racist in history. That should leave us questioning any judgment or analysis that just happens to coincide with ideas rooted in our racist past.

An alternative is to suggest that high rates of unemployment for black Americans, high rates of incarceration, and low rates of educational success are a systemic problem in the culture that white Americans created. Does the average black person in America start on a level playing field? Can one attribute our indices of shame to lower levels of black ability and ambition? Is that negative view consistent with the tremendous effort and ability shown by black athletes and black entertainers in America? Is it consistent with the reality that African Americans invented jazz and blues, two musical forms that have spread around the world for a century, and that black music inspired early rock stars—Elvis Presley, the Beatles, the Rolling Stones—and the entire phenomenon of rock and roll? Can it be reconciled with the intelligence of scholars like Henry Louis Gates, Jr., and Cornel West, or the brilliance of writers like Alice Walker and Toni Morrison? Does it make sense of Barack Obama, who is very often the smartest person in the room? Does it make sense of Michelle Obama, who is right there with him?

An honest assessment almost certainly must conclude that low rates of African-American success in education and in the American economy, plus high rates of entanglement in our criminal justice system are rooted in nearly three centuries of slavery and one additional century of extreme racial prejudice. Is it not then an American obligation to focus upon and try to resolve this ongoing and unacceptable injustice? By one measure, our civil rights heritage, fostered by Martin Luther King and an entire generation of activists and idealists, is one of the greatest accomplishments of modern America. We Americans have managed to beat back racism and nurture the rise of a black middle class in ways that inspire observers throughout the world. We should be proud of that. If white Americans also listen to those who think we now live in a just, post-racial society, with no lingering heritage from our racist past, it will betray what is best about this nation. There is more to be done. The left has always been right, and it is right on race today.

CHAPTER 4: MONEY

Some say that all political questions are really about money. That might be an exaggeration. However, Bill Clinton won two terms in the White House by repeating one mantra, "It's the economy, stupid." Furthermore, the American economy entering the second decade of the twenty-first century grabs our attention because it is in serious trouble. The Great Recession that hit the United States and spread throughout the world in 2008 represents the steepest economic decline and our worst economic nightmare since the Great Depression of the 1930s. It has created hardship, anxiety, and anger.

In the fall of 2011 the Occupy Wall Street movement developed, showing some of that anger and capturing national and international attention by holding up signs with one simple message, "We are the 99%." Ninety-nine percent of the American public is suffering from this economy. That 99% has actually suffered for three full decades, especially when compared to the other 1%. According to a recent Congressional Budget Office report, the top 1% in America has seen its share of after-tax national income more than double from less than 8% in 1979 to 17% in 2007. The top 20% now earn 53% of national income, so that the bottom 80% earns less than half. The lowest 20% of Americans saw their share of after-tax income drop from 7% to 5%. All of these data confirm a growing gap between rich and poor in America, and the CBO report concludes that government tax policy has contributed to the trend. Receiving the lion's share of increased income and the lion's share of lowered taxes, the extremely rich have done very well in Ronald Reagan and George W. Bush's America. Unfortunately, that top 1% is virtually the only group that has done well. Middle class Americans have seen minor gains over thirty years, with many of those gains now lost or under threat. A majority of the population is relatively worse off today than the day Reagan brought Republican economics into the White House.

If we consider our unemployment numbers, hovering at 9% through 2011, we recognize that figure as a result of the Great Recession. But job shortages also reflect more deep-seated problems. While Bill Clinton was in office—focusing on his "It's the economy, stupid" message—he created 23 million jobs. George W. Bush also spent two full terms in office and he created one million jobs! Those numbers suggest a wrong turn somewhere. The stock market provides another indicator of something gone wrong. It used to be said that stocks will bounce up and down, but should earn 10% per year over time. During the first decade of this century, however, the Dow Jones Average started at 11,497 and ended the decade just over 10,000. By November 2011 it hovered between 11,500 and 12,000, almost exactly where it had begun the century. By contrast, Bill Clinton inherited a Dow Jones Average at 3,200 and left it over 10,000. Other presidents also presided over a rising stock market. Again, something seems to have gone wrong under the second George Bush.

Our national economic pain includes a large and growing national debt. This debt is a major focus for Tea Party rage and a focal point for Republican rhetoric. It is worth noting, therefore, that a huge portion of that debt can also be traced to George W. Bush. He inherited from Bill Clinton a national debt of $5.8 trillion, *along with a balanced budget and a projection that the entire national debt would be paid off within less than two decades!* That was our standard assumption in 2000. After eight years in office, Bush handed Barack Obama a debt that had nearly doubled to $10.627 trillion. He also handed off a budget wildly out of balance and an economic crisis that is almost entirely responsible for the approximately $5 trillion by which our national debt has increased under Obama. (See a closer analysis of the present economic crisis later in this chapter.)

It is wrong, of course, to suggest that our national debt crisis is primarily George W. Bush's fault. He has every right to share the blame with his father, the first President Bush, and with Ronald Reagan. Of the $10.627 trillion in national debt passed on to the Obama presidency, they created a total of $8.16 trillion. In other words, our last three Republican presidents combined for nearly 80% of the national debt handed to the Democrat, Barack Obama, in 2009. Republicans should not be allowed to talk about our national debt without some acknowledgement of these startling numbers, numbers that shed important and undeniable light on where the fault actually lies. These figures highlight the extreme hypocrisy of the standard Republican rhetoric on "tax and spend Democrats."

The hypocrisy of Republican rhetoric, as indicated by a look at actual numbers, does point us toward another part of our problem. We are suffering not just from our present economy but from some very bad economic ideas. These are the rightwing ideas handed to George W. Bush that he then pushed throughout his term in office. He thought the answer to every problem was to lower taxes, especially on the rich. He spoke of the job creation that would grow out of tax cuts, as Republicans always do. But the record speaks for itself. Bill Clinton raised taxes, balanced the budget, and created 23 million jobs. George W Bush lowered taxes dramatically, dramatically increased our national debt, and he created 22 million fewer jobs than Clinton!

Reality-based history suggests that today's Republican ideas on the economy are simply wrong. One of those underlying ideas involves an almost religious belief in free market capitalism, the laissez-faire version, where we tell the government to "leave it alone." Some people extol the free market as if it were sliced bread. If you will excuse a second culinary metaphor, it is in reality chopped liver. Capitalism produces some quite good results, but free market, laissez-faire capitalism simply does not work the way its most enthusiastic supporters claim. In fact, it has had to be sliced and chopped, cut back and regulated in order to make it work in an acceptable manner at all. European nations did that in the twentieth century. We did that in the twentieth century. There are differences in degree and approach in modern, rich countries around the world, but every successful nation controls and regulates capitalism. Otherwise, we could not stand to live with the results. To talk about free market capitalism today as if it really exists is factually wrong. Every market is regulated. "Deregulation" as a slogan is wrongheaded. As policy it makes no sense, unless we pay attention to how and why our system requires regulation. Then we can begin an intelligent discussion about which regulations make sense and which do not.

    The second really bad Republican idea involves taxes. Republicans since Ronald Reagan have found they can win elections by promising to lower taxes. Shortsighted voters drink the Kool-Aid, which means they vote to lower taxes, either directly by initiative and referendum or indirectly by supporting politicians who run on an anti-tax platform. Everyone forgets in this game of blind man's bluff that there is no free lunch. The lunch we get is a lunch for which we pay, or a lunch for which our children pay. Federal tax revenues are at their lowest level in relation to GDP since the 1950s. Our anti-tax mania has caused problems in the present, as well as for the future. That includes our corrosive national debt, with a growing portion of our annual budget going toward debt repayment. We also have more potholes in our roads and we have dangerous bridges, just two example of our degraded infrastructure. We have reduced investment in education in general and in higher education in particular, with increasingly restricted access for the poor; and we have significantly reduced assistance for the poorest members of our society across the board. Despite these cuts made around the edges of our national budget, no Republicans have been willing to vote against major government programs, those which benefit farmers, the elderly, the middle class, or, above all, the military. The result is a budget in which Ronald Reagan, George H.W. Bush, and George W. Bush are by far the most careless spenders in our entire history, as noted above. That might seem ironic to an outside observer. The Republican Party, which most talks about fiscal responsibility, has put us in an absolute sinkhole of national debt.

    These really bad ideas about the wonders of free market capitalism and lower taxes have come to dominate rightwing politics in America. Republicans used to be able to have a reality-based conversation on economic issues. They used to be willing to consider data and evidence. That is why there used to be moderate Republicans. That is why George H. W. Bush in 1980 was willing to label Reagan's misguided ideas as "voodoo economics." That is why even Speaker of the House John Boehner stayed somewhere within the universe of reason during the summer of 2011 debt-ceiling negotiations. But he stayed there only until he discovered that the crucial votes in his caucus did not reside within the universe of reason. For today's Republicans, reality is not allowed to impinge. They have become a faith-based party on economics as well as evolution. That is why we must begin by confronting their faith-based assumptions.

On faith in Capitalism and faith in the Bible

At the risk of giving offense, it seems necessary to point out two realities: Capitalism does not work and the Bible is not true. Certain groups in our nation base their entire outlook in life on the opposite set of claims—that free market capitalism works perfectly and that every word in the Bible is absolutely true. Often the person who believes fervently in capitalism and the person who believes fervently in the Bible is the same person. Sometimes a person believes primarily in capitalism and is skeptical about the Bible. This happens quite often. There might be a few Americans who believe in an inerrant Bible and are skeptical about capitalism, though I have never met one. One thing I do know is that most people in this country who believe in one or both of these "absolute truths" place themselves on the political right and they vote Republican. It is important to open our eyes and recognize that they are wrong.

Analyzing these two "faith systems" is especially important in today's America, since rightwing Republicans have made fervent belief in absolute truths the essence and cornerstone of their politics. Reasonably educated and intelligent people who run for president as Republicans have to travel the country saying things they know to be untrue, or else they have no chance of wooing the Republican base. So I will begin this chapter by pointing out that these two shibboleths in the world of American ideas are both simply wrong. We can try to use our intelligence when we discuss them, rather than just close our eyes and shout very loudly.

Let's begin with the Bible. It is an important book and a beautifully written book. With certain variations, it is the foundation for three important religions—Judaism, Christianity, and Islam. Each of these religions can be perfectly useful and respectable, providing ethical guidance and making possible a harmonious, meaningful life. Any one of us can be born into one of these religions, or convert to one of them, and become convinced that it is the best religion of all, or even the one true religion. It is even possible that one group might be correct in making this claim. Maybe Judaism, Christianity, or Islam really is the best religion, or even the one true religion. An intelligent, educated person can accept all of the above statements and possibilities without too much difficulty. We can be agnostic when we get to the outer edges of what claims might be true. But no intelligent, educated person can accept that the Bible is *absolutely* true. There are too many mistakes. There are too many inconsistencies. And there are too many portions that everyone chooses to ignore, even those who claim to believe absolutely in every word.

Christians who want to test my claim can look at the genealogy of Jesus as mentioned in the Gospels of Matthew and Luke. They simply do not match. The names are all wrong and out of order. Jews can look at the ethic of a God who endorses polygamy, or a God who orders the Israelites to kill every last human being and farm animal in the land he has given them. These are interesting tales from the past, but not acceptable as an appropriate ethic for today. Christians who oppose gay rights cite a verse in the Book of Leviticus. It calls a man lying down with a man an "abomination," which they then claim represents an absolute and unequivocal ban on homosexuality. However, these same Christians dismiss all of the other abominations mentioned in Leviticus—eating shellfish, eating pork, shaving—with the blithe comment that Jesus has made such restrictions obsolete. Most of these same Christians also ignore the New Testament passage where Paul tells women not to use cosmetics, and virtually all of these Christians ignore Jesus' request to take all that they have and give it to the poor.

No one uses the Bible without picking and choosing. The problem arises when some people still claim that every word in the Bible is literally true. Worse yet, they are likely to claim that these "infallible" words fit exactly into the interpretation they choose to give them today. Many Christians throughout history have been able to read the book of Genesis and understand the six-day creation as a metaphor. They see a story proclaiming God's creative power and purpose. When some Christians today focus on the six-day creation as if it were science—including, of necessity, those Christians who choose to ignore or creatively reinterpret many other claims or messages in the same Bible—that is when they find themselves forced to ignore science entirely. It has them visiting a "Creation Museum" in Kentucky, a museum claiming that dinosaurs coexisted with humans, despite scientific claims to the contrary. This museum even displays a dinosaur wearing a saddle. It is a losing battle and it makes Christians look silly.

Now let's switch to another religion in today's America: Capitalism. We learned in this country more than a century ago that laissez faire capitalism does not work. Late-nineteenth-century America produced one capitalist abuse after another, the sort of things that the American voter finally would not accept. It produced corruption, with capitalists buying politicians and judges whenever they could. It produced unsafe working conditions, in which those who were killed or dismembered were simply sent home or sent to the morgue. A lost worker was easily replaced by the next immigrant desperate for work. Capitalists hired children, because they could be paid a fraction of the wage of an adult, and they imposed long hours and low wages on everyone according to the "laws of the free market." Worst of all, perhaps, free market capitalism produced monopoly, allowing the most successful capitalists to leave competition behind entirely. A monopolist can gouge the consumer and underpay the worker, with no fear that he will be undersold or out-recruited by a competitor. That is what we learned more than a century ago. Mark Twain labeled that period a "Gilded Age," with the shiny look of gold merely a thin veneer, hiding the base metal underneath. The Gilded Age of the late nineteenth century led to populism and then to the Progressive Era, a time when we began to do some surgery on free market capitalism for the national good.

In the last three decades our worship of capitalism has led to renewed capitalist abuses. Our present century began with the Enron scandal, in which a few rich people gouged the public and then obliterated the jobs and pensions of their workers. We have had the subprime mortgage crisis, in which banks, bankers, and Wall Street financiers learned how to make massive amounts of money in a clever manner, but with the small downside that they crashed the international economy and created the worst economic crisis since the Great Depression. We have had the Ponzi scheme of Bernie Madoff, who stole the money of otherwise intelligent people whose greed for high returns fed Madoff's greed for massive returns of his own.

Why do these things happen? Capitalists make money wherever they can and however they can. They might try to soften this reality be claiming their job is to make money for their stockholders, not just for themselves. A few capitalists, the really soft-hearted ones, might actually have a personal ethic that prevents them from preying upon children, the elderly, or other vulnerable victims. But they will likely be replaced when the numbers do not add up. There is always a "Chainsaw Al" (or a Mitt Romney), a "vulture capitalist" ready to step in and improve the numbers by selling off, by laying off, or by crunching things some other way to save the bottom line. *There is absolutely no morality, no ethic in textbook capitalism, and we are wrong to imagine that there is.* The only thing that normally will prevent a hard-headed capitalist from employing a hardball tactic is a set of laws that regulate and limit the free market, along with a threat of corporate or personal liability.

We have decided as a nation that certain tactics should be illegal, tactics such as insider trading, where some can manipulate the market for their advantage and the rest of us are set up to lose money. We have decided that certain protections should be in place for the potential victims of capitalism: consumers, workers, investors, the environment, the economy as a whole. We came to this conclusion during the twentieth century, as did the entire rest of the industrial world! All modern nations created a body of laws to limit the methods and the greed of capitalists. When capitalists violate one or more of these laws, they might even go to jail. That happened to Bernie Madoff and to a couple of Enron executives. That is our way to protect ourselves against the worst abuses. When capitalists behave in ways most of us might find unethical, but which violate no law, they please their investors. "There is no law against it," they say, as they smile their way to the bank. Our only protection is to write an intelligent set of laws against unfair, unethical, exploitative capitalist behavior and then enforce those laws.

To imagine that some pure version of free market capitalism is an answer to today's problems is absurd. To think we can or should get rid of regulation is absurd. The lessons of well over a century teach us that free market capitalism does not work. It is not acceptable. The only real question is how we should regulate business, not whether it should be regulated. Our task is to create a web of laws and regulations that balances the energy and creativity of capitalism with protection for the rest of us. We have a right as a democratic nation to protect our consumers, our workers, our investors, and the national economy as a whole. We should do so intelligently, without being blinded by a statement of faith that turns free market capitalism into a religion.

Adam Smith and his "invisible hand"

Adam Smith was a moral philosopher who wrote the book on capitalism. On the economic side, he saw the problem of medieval guilds, authoritarian governments, and outdated laws that impeded the flow and creativity of the new industrial and capitalist methods. His *Wealth of Nations*, published in 1776, told us to let it flow. On the moral philosophy side, he told us that greed is good. He also created an apparatus that connected the two ideas, including his invention of a ghost in the works, "the invisible hand."

To make the claim in Christian Scotland in the eighteenth century that greed is good was quite revolutionary. Greed is thoroughly deplored in the Bible. "The love of money is the root of all evil," the Bible says. "Take all that you have and give it to the poor," Jesus said. He also said it is "easier for a camel to get through the eye of a needle than for a rich man to enter the kingdom of heaven." The Israelites celebrated a year of jubilee every 75 years, in which all debts were forgiven. As Jim Wallis of *Sojourners* magazine has said, if you take compassion for the poor out of the Bible, you are left with a pamphlet.

All three monotheistic religions, the religions rooted in the Jewish Bible, have a very deep-seated tradition that to be greedy is to be sinful. Adam Smith attacked that idea so successfully that an American preacher in the Gilded Age, Russell Conwell, could get rich himself by giving a sermon 6000 times called "Acres of Diamonds." Real Christians will prosper, he said. Some Christians today tell you to attach a picture of a Cadillac or a yacht or a waterfront mansion in Florida to your refrigerator, to show you what God has in store for you. Just believe. Very few Christians today see Capitalism and Christianity at odds with each other. Adam Smith played a very large role in that change.

Greed, according to Smith, is the engine that drives the economy, and that is good. It nurtures creativity. It inspires ambition. It should be unimpeded. The beauty of this freedom to indulge our greed, in Smith's theory, is that the end result will be good for everyone, not just for the rich and successful. He reached that happy conclusion by looking at the law of supply and demand, coupled with free competition. He then concluded that a benign "invisible hand" will ensure the fairest and most appropriate outcome for all of us in terms of the wages we earn and the prices we pay. If some entrepreneur is selling shoes for $100 a pair, even if they cost him only $20 a pair to produce, that evidence of greed is perfectly okay. With free competition, others will see his enormous profit, enter the market, and undersell him, perhaps at $80 a pair. Eventually, competitors will drive that price down, perhaps to $21 a pair, and the customer will get the best shoes at the best price. The invisible hand of competition drove the supply up and the price down until the customer got a fair deal and the entrepreneur earned merely a fair return. If the entrepreneur gets discouraged at his lowered rate of return, he will turn elsewhere, perhaps to blue jeans, and start the process all over again.

According to Smith's theory, the same invisible hand should create fair wages and working conditions. If the supply of workers is low, let's say in Alaska as the pipeline was being built, or among civilian contractors in Iraq or Afghanistan today, the wages will have to be high enough to attract workers to the job. That temporary dislocation—too good for the workers and too harsh for the employer—will change according to the laws of supply and demand, plus the benefit of free competition. Other workers will hear about the good money and move to Alaska or sign up for Iraq, and the wages and conditions will soon reach the fairest possible level.

We now know that the market is not nearly as fluid as Adam Smith's theory suggests. For example, workers suffering from low wages in one place are not always able to move someplace else. They cannot sell their house, perhaps, or they do not want to leave family and friends. In the worst cases, they have no car and cannot afford a ticket for the bus. During the Great Depression, many would-be workers without a car or a bus ticket hopped a freight. They could travel from one region of the country to another by riding the rails, but they could not find a place where the supply of workers did not far outstrip the demand. In their case, the invisible hand of equity let them down. Another problem can be seen in late-nineteenth-century America, when an influx of immigrants arrived in a nation with rapidly expanding factories. For an extended period, the supply of desperate immigrants exceeded the demand in factories. In accord with the laws of the free market, steel workers, for example, found themselves working twelve hours a day, seven days per week, at wages that barely provided food and shelter for themselves, much less a family. Profits might have been high, but any owner paying attention to supply and demand had no incentive to pay wages higher than an amount that would attract the necessary number of workers.

Another problem in free market competition became noticeable when we learned that capitalists do not really like competition. The most successful competitors, people like John D. Rockefeller, the ones really good at the game, strive to beat back their competitors until the competitors no longer exist. Then the game is up and the monopolist has his way. The story of transcontinental railroads in 1860s America makes for a good example, and it includes an interesting sidebar on socialism for the rich. No entrepreneur was willing to undertake the tremendous cost of land acquisition and construction for a railroad to California, Oregon, or Washington, especially because potential customers were so thinly dispersed that revenues could not be assured. Congress decided to subsidize these entrepreneurs, giving them the land on which to lay their tracks, plus large amounts of land adjoining the railway, plus large amounts of cash for every mile of track completed. One result was graft and corruption. It is now estimated that two of every three dollars spent on the construction of our transcontinental railways was stolen or misappropriated. Another result was that railroad companies became huge landowners, acquiring one-half the land adjacent to their tracks in a checkerboard swath as wide as 80 miles in the case of the Northern Pacific. This land granted to the railroads was also the most valuable land in the West, since it was closest to a transportation link. That points toward the final result of the transcontinental railways: a monopoly relationship with their customers.

Railroads in the nineteenth-century West illustrate the pricing concept of "all the market will bear." Homesteaders moved to North Dakota, for example, on the promise that they could acquire free land, grow wheat, ship their wheat to Minneapolis by rail, and become rich. They got their land. They grew their wheat. And then they faced the shipping costs set by the Northern Pacific. It is important to notice that the shipping price would not be based upon the cost to the railroad, plus a "fair" rate of return. That is not free market capitalism. If wheat was selling in Minneapolis for 25 cents a bushel, the railroad had to decide whether to charge 10 cents, 15 cents, or perhaps 24 cents a bushel to ship it. At a certain point, the farmers would be happy. That meant the price was too low. At a certain point the farmers would become so angry they would rather burn their wheat in the field. That meant the price was too high. If the farmers moaned at the price and got red in the face with anger, but still decided it was worth shipping their wheat and earning a meager return, then the price was just right. It was normal for farmers to hate the railroads, and it was normal for them to be trapped. They could not possibly transport their wheat to Minneapolis in their own wagons. The value/bulk ratio was all wrong and the time involved impossible. They also could not get their wheat to an alternative transcontinental. Finally, it was not reasonable to imagine building more transcontinental railroads to create local competition. The cost was too high and the waste would have been formidable. Since 1887 and the creation of the Interstate Commerce Commission (though with mixed results at first), the free market in railroad rates has been taken away for the common good. The same is true for many other natural monopolies, such as the supply of water or the supply of electricity. As a society we have often suffered from price-gouging by these natural monopolies, and we have responded by insisting that government intervene.

Another pattern in monopoly can be seen in the career of John D. Rockefeller and his Standard Oil Company. Rockefeller was very good at creating economies of scale while acquiring and refining oil and selling the final product. This meant that smaller companies could not match his price. For example, Rockefeller made agreements with railroads to grant him a rebate on every barrel of oil he shipped. Because of the volume of his business, he could get this secret (and illegal) rebate, while other oil companies paid the listed rate. If necessary, Rockefeller was also willing to engage in a price war. Say that kerosene cost him a certain amount to produce, perhaps 10 cents per gallon. He might enter the market in Georgia and sell it for 8 cents per gallon. Given his vast capital resources, he could afford to lose money on every gallon sold for as long as necessary. Smaller competitors could leave their price where it was, perhaps at 12 cents per gallon, and lose their customers to Rockefeller. Alternatively, they could enter the price war and lose money on every gallon. No small competitor could afford to lose as much as Rockefeller, however, so this was a war he always would win. When he had destroyed the competitor, or perhaps purchased the competitor at a fire-sale price, customers in that region discovered that their brief period of low prices had proved very expensive in the long run. With a monopoly of supply, Rockefeller could charge "all the market would bear," raising his price until people simply decided to quit using kerosene. Then he would drop the price a penny or two. Of course, if customers could have relied on Rockefeller passing all of his economies of scale to them in lower prices, his expertise and methods would have been to their advantage. But why would he do that? If there was no law against his tactics and if there was no competitor still in place, he only had to follow the law of supply and demand. That meant gouging his customers to raise his profit. Who would not?

Andrew Carnegie and the "American System" of business management
Rockefeller, Cornelius Vanderbilt, and many other rich Americans in the late-nineteenth century became known as the "Robber Barons." However, they not only stole their wealth (or, in many cases, earned it with methods that would be illegal or seem unethical today), they also gave wealth back to the American economy in the form of jobs, good products, and low prices. It was not all bad. The career of Andrew Carnegie (as told, for example, by Harold Livesay in *Andrew Carnegie and the Rise of Big Business*) provides especially useful evidence on the two sides to this story. In the first stage of his career, he became very wealthy, based upon hard work, quick intelligence, good fortune, and a series of tactics that would be mostly illegal today. Then, between 1870 and 1900, he became the largest and best steelmaker in the world. He also carried the American steel business on his shoulders, so that during that time the United States became the largest steelmaker in the world. Furthermore, the production of steel at that stage of the industrial revolution was the best single indicator of national success. It provided the most important product for major elements in a modern economy: railroads, bridges, steel beam skyscrapers, and, very soon, the automobile industry. When the United States became the richest nation in the world, it would have been unimaginable without steel; and Andrew Carnegie led the way as the world's best steelmaker.

Carnegie might be the most complete story of rags to riches in American history. In contrast to many or most entrepreneurs, he really did start out in poverty. When Andrew arrived in Pittsburgh in 1848 at the age of thirteen, it was because his father had gone bankrupt in Scotland, continuing to weave cloth by hand when machines had begun to take over the industry. The family had to borrow money to get to America and they had to take up meager jobs to get their start. Andrew earned $1.20 a week, working six days and 72 hours in a textile factory at a little less than 2 cents an hour. He also started

The Left Has Always Been Right

night school, learning double-entry bookkeeping. He soon got a job as a messenger boy in a telegraph office and then learned telegraphy. When Tom Scott of the Pennsylvania Railroad recognized the importance of rapid communication in the train business, he decided that his personal secretary should know telegraphy. Looking for the best telegrapher in Pittsburgh, he found Andrew Carnegie. At the age of seventeen, Andrew's rapid rise to wealth had begun.

Tom Scott, superintendent of the western division of the Pennsylvania Railroad, was an important man, second only to J. Edgar Thomson, the company president. During the 1850s and early 1860s, they established the Pennsylvania Railroad as the best managed and most successful railroad in the world. That involved management techniques observed by Carnegie that he later applied to the steel business. He also learned from Scott and Thomson how to get rich. They were good at creating revenue for investors in their railroad. They were also very good at using their insiders' position to create wealth for themselves. They would invest in a company that made sleeping cars, for example, or built bridges. Then they would make sure that the Pennsylvania Railroad bought those sleeping cars or used those bridges. In all cases, Thomson and Scott would hide their ownership—that is, their conflict of interest—by having Carnegie buy the stock, and they would include him as a co-investor. It was practically like printing money.

Carnegie bought his first stock for $600 in 1856 at the age of twenty-one. He bought it on the recommendation of Tom Scott and with money loaned to him by Scott. By 1863 the annual dividend from that first stock was $1440. If a 10% return on a stock is good, say $60/year in this case, a return of $1440 per year must be considered better than good! These numbers and their implications are worth exploring a bit. By the age of twenty-four, Carnegie had risen to Tom Scott's old job, superintendent of the western division of the Pennsylvania Railroad, with Scott promoted to general superintendent. Carnegie was now paid $2400 per year. By the age of twenty-eight, he also earned $45,000 per year on his stock portfolio, based on an original investment of $817 of borrowed money. By the age of thirty-three he earned $56,000 per year on a portfolio worth $400,000. After his first investment, he played only with his winnings and he did extremely well.

If we try to determine the value of the youthful Carnegie's income in today's dollar, there is no absolute measurement. However, we can keep the math simple and multiply these figures by 100. That gives Carnegie an income of $240,000 per year when he was the highest executive under Thomson and Scott in the world's most successful railroad. That hardly seems too high an estimate and might, in fact, be too low. But that multiple of 100 then raises his investment income at the age of twenty-eight to $4.5 million per year. By the age of thirty-three, his portfolio was worth $40 million and his annual income from investments was $5.6 million.

While growing enormously rich on his stocks, Carnegie used the coattails of Thomson and Scott for one more side career. It took relatively little time and yet was the most lucrative of all. Someone had to carry St. Louis Bridge bonds to London in 1869 to try to sell them to a broker. Thomson and Scott sent Carnegie, along with their letters of recommendation. For an afternoon's work in London, he made $50,000 (in his dollars). In approximately five years he arranged $30 million in bond sales, earning a fee which averaged 2.5%. That would be $750,000 in five years or $150,000 per year, with a work load that often meant a trans-Atlantic holiday along with a one or two-day meeting with a broker. Using our multiple of 100/1, that gave him an income of $15 million per year for five years, on top of his $5.6 million per year off of stocks, plus his salary of $240,000 as a top executive at the Pennsylvania Railroad. Though that executive salary was generous, he hardly would have noticed whether it reached his bank account or not. And, by the way, this was before anyone in America paid income tax.

Carnegie broke no laws in amassing his fortune. He relied upon his intelligence, his charm, and his connection to two powerful men. When they made money, he made money. One might even think that no one was hurt by their game. However, they occasionally manipulated a stock by controlling news or controlling board decisions. Then, when the moment was right, they used their insider information to sell for a profit and leave other investors holding an empty

The Left Has Always Been Right

bag. That is why insider trading is now illegal. As for the leverage they had by way of the Pennsylvania Railroad, one must assume that stockholders in that company were hurt by Thomson and Scott's antics. These two had a personal interest in choosing vendors for the railroad in which they secretly held stock. Accepting the lowest bid was never their primary concern in such decisions. In fact, overpaying a vendor or a subcontracting company in which they held stock meant a higher dividend for them from that stock. The Pennsylvania Railroad was so successful that investors did not protest (nor did they know, of course). However, the railroad's profits and dividends would have been higher if Thomson and Scott had maximized efficiency, rather than personal benefit. That is why they hid their names and purchased their stocks through the younger and less widely known Carnegie. It is worth noting that Carnegie, when he owned Carnegie Steel, would fire an employee who put personal profit ahead of company efficiency.

If the young Andrew Carnegie who grew extravagantly rich were the only Carnegie we knew, he would elicit some respect, some envy, and relatively little admiration. He himself wrote a critical self-assessment at that stage of his career:

> Thirty three and an income of 50,000$ per annum.... [Then, after mentioning a goal of retiring within two years and starting to give away his money, he added,] The amassing of wealth is one of the worst species of idolatry. No idol more debasing than the worship of money.... To continue much longer overwhelmed by business cares and with most of my thoughts wholly upon the way to make more money in the shortest time, must degrade me beyond hope of permanent recovery.

Carnegie worked another thirty-two years, rather than two, and he made massive amounts of additional money. When he sold Carnegie Steel in 1901, he was worth about $400 million and was probably the richest man in the world. Using again the 100/1 ratio, this might have been $40 billion in today's dollars. Carnegie really did give away his fortune, leaving behind Carnegie Hall, Carnegie-Mellon University, Carnegie libraries throughout the United States and Great Britain, and the Carnegie Foundation. He also transformed American business, giving us all a primer on how to run a company for maximum efficiency.

When Carnegie got into the steel business, dabbling in the 1860s and starting Carnegie Steel in 1872, Great Britain had the largest and best steel production in the world and steel rails cost $300 per ton. Within thirty years Carnegie produced more steel than all of Great Britain, and he had driven the price down to $11 per ton. That was good for him and good for the United States. It was also good for the entire industrial world, since the ability to purchase cheap steel made so many other ventures possible. He accomplished this success by inventing and/or applying a series of management techniques that have been taught in business schools ever since. Measure everything. Reward success. Reinvest. Work toward long-term results.

Carnegie learned about numbers from Thomson and Scott at the Pennsylvania Railroad. A few numbers written into logbooks at the end of every workday and then compiled by the week, the month, the quarter, and the year, could tell him which worker feeding a blast furnace accomplished the most and which regional manager produced the best results. This required massive paperwork, which "wasted time," and it required many accountants, who produced no steel but had to be paid. But it also made every management decision simple. You no longer needed to think of workers or managers as individuals—a relative, perhaps, or a friend—but you could see them as numbers. Your job was to promote the successful ones and fire the others. The same numbers would allow you to make rational investment choices, rather than follow your gut instincts. Carnegie hired a chemist, which seemed like wasted money to other steelmakers; but his chemist could tell him the exact iron content of ore from various mines, taking the guesswork out of assessments by color, feel, or reputation and pushing the iron-per-ton-of-ore ratio in his favor. On one occasion Carnegie "wasted" money by dismantling a newly constructed steel mill, having learned that more efficient equipment had just been developed. Bean counters could tell him how much it would cost to throw out the brand new and entirely serviceable equipment, how much it would cost to install the new equipment, how much they could expect to save per year, and how long it would take to recoup their investment. Carnegie quickly decided that he could not afford to produce steel with inferior equipment and he made the change.

"Bean counter" tends to be a term of reproach in today's America, even though accountants were at the heart of Carnegie's management system. For example, when the Ford Motor Company realized that a Ford Pinto design flaw could result in an exploding gas tank, they turned the problem over to their bean counters. Estimating how many people might be burned to a crisp in such accidents and how much each settlement might cost, Ford accountants allegedly determined that the company would likely pay less in settlements than in retooling and refitting the car. That is a normal business practice and it might have seemed a good business decision, but it probably underestimated the outrage factor in today's America as well as our culture of public safety laws. A Hollywood film, *Class Action* (1991), based itself on the Pinto case and thus added to the ethical stain on Ford's logo and the negative reputation of corporate accountants.

In Carnegie's day factory owners faced similar questions, but with no legal restraint whatsoever and before a culture of outrage had developed. For example, if a piece of dangerous equipment might occasionally entangle a worker and cut off an arm or, depending on the bite, shred a worker entirely, an accountant could give two cost comparisons. Safety equipment would cost a certain amount to install and might also impede the pace of production to a certain extent. Balanced against that option would be the choice not to install safety equipment. That would mean lost time of production when accidents occurred and the equipment had to be shut down. It also meant wages expended on someone cleaning up the blood, gore, and body parts smearing the equipment, and the expense required to hire and to train a replacement worker. The factory owner had no financial obligation for medical expenses, a funeral, or the care and feeding of the worker's dependents. By Carnegie's methods of management—entirely acceptable in economic terms—safety equipment would almost never be installed. It was not cost effective. Only government safety laws have changed that reality.

Whenever the cost-benefit analysis suggested a good economic return, of course, Carnegie was likely to invest. In fact, reinvestment was one of the most important elements in his business success. All capitalists face a choice when their business makes a profit of what to do with that profit. Paying large dividends is popular with investors. Quarterly profits and quarterly dividends are watched and appreciated by investors to this day. Carnegie, however, always voted in favor of using corporate profits primarily for reinvestment, rather than large dividends. That is to say, he preferred long-term benefit to short-term benefit. Two factors helped him take this approach. First of all, he owned more than half the stock, so his vote at board meetings was the only one that counted. Secondly, he owned so much stock that even a small dividend put plenty of income in his pocket. For nearly thirty years Carnegie reinvested in the newest and best equipment and processes, with the result that he always was ahead of his competitors. He also integrated his business vertically, buying control of the newly discovered Mesabi iron ore deposits in Minnesota, merging the Henry Frick Coke Works with Carnegie Steel, building the boats to carry raw materials across the Great Lakes, and building his own railroad to transport raw materials and finished product within his empire. It gave him tremendous efficiency and constantly reduced his cost per ton of steel.

In the 1890s a group of steel makers tried to make a deal with Carnegie, suggesting an iron and steel trust under a single ownership group. The idea involved sharing the market in predetermined percentages, rather than competing by price. The real goal was to make sure that the individual companies did not have to continue to lower their prices to match Carnegie. Competition such as that required expensive investments in new equipment and it lowered dividends for themselves and their stockholders. The consumer, of course, would be the one paying for the inefficiencies of a trust, their high prices and their high dividends. Carnegie's partners would have been very pleased to start tapping the revenues of their very successful company. He, however, rejected the idea and made plans for yet another massive investment, so that Carnegie Steel could produce end products, such as wire or boilers, hoops or nails. That would avoid the danger

The Left Has Always Been Right

that an integrated trust, including many of Carnegie's customers for steel bars or steel plate, would quit purchasing his steel, even though it was cheapest and best. By 1901 Andrew Carnegie was 65 years old and the American banker, J.P. Morgan, was eager to "stabilize" the steel industry. He arranged the purchase of Carnegie Steel for $480 million and created U.S. Steel, essentially the sort of trust that Carnegie had previously rejected. The American steel industry has never been so efficient since.

One additional factor might have made Carnegie ready to sell by 1901. That was the violent Homestead Strike of 1992, which left four dead, many injured, and Carnegie's reputation as a friend of workers in tatters. He always had tried to maintain a humanitarian image while building his wealth in the harsh world of business. He wrote *The Gospel of Wealth* (1889), for example, which suggested that the acquisition of wealth was only legitimate if one then gave it away to good causes. He also spoke about fairness for workers. He even defended the right of workers to form unions, which put him far outside the corporate mainstream of his day. On one occasion he developed a three-shift system for his steelworkers. This would employ three shifts working eight hours per day and seven days per week, rather than the industry norm of two shifts working twelve hours per day. However, Carnegie's mania for cutting costs could hardly leave workers' hours and wages safe from his scalpel. The eight-hour shift fell by the wayside. Then in 1892, when Carnegie Steel was making record profits, the labor contract at his Homestead Works came up for renewal. Carnegie could not resist using the leverage of supply and demand. He decided he could lower wages and break the union by offering a take-it-or-leave-it deal.

Carnegie and his partners recognized that his soft spot might resurface if he were the one having to face down the workers at Homestead. Therefore, he left for Scotland after placing Henry Frick, his toughest and most anti-labor partner, in complete charge. Frick fortified the steel mill with watchtowers, rifle slits, and barbed wire and made plans to bring in 300 well-armed Pinkerton agents on barges under cover of night to lock down the site. He then hoped to reopen with non-union, strikebreaking workers willing to accept his offer on wages and conditions. Workers discovered the Pinkertons, however, and met them at the water's edge, leading to a fierce, daylong battle. Eight thousand troops were sent the next day to give government support to management. Union workers then lost at least part of the public relations battle when someone—not one of their own—shot and stabbed Frick in an assassination attempt. Frick survived, he lowered wages, and he broke the union, but Carnegie lost face. With his retirement in 1901, he undertook philanthropy in earnest, tilting toward the good-guy side of his image for the last eighteen years of his life.

Both Rockefeller and Carnegie illustrate the truth that free market capitalism leads almost inevitably toward monopoly. The best producers maximize efficiency and gain economies of scale. In the end, they are likely to dominate an entire industry. The widespread development of trusts in America in the 1890s represents a variation on monopoly in which all major producers merge so as not to compete. Trusts developed in almost every industry in that decade. Because trusts are designed primarily to reduce investment, raise prices, and gouge the consumer, "trust busting" became a popular part of Teddy Roosevelt's persona and an ongoing part of the federal government's role for more than a century. This is one more indicator that free market capitalism does not work, no matter what conservatives say about free markets today. Intelligent regulation is our only choice.

Government and the economy

As noted above, government control and regulation of business to maximize fairness and protect us from various forms of harm is an acknowledged necessity. No serious person would recommend that we get rid of regulation, even if many talk blithely about the free market and all its virtues. The same is true in terms of our government and macroeconomics. The Great Depression of the 1930s gives us our best lesson about the government's role in the economy, and certain aspects of that lesson are quite simple. One truth is that government intervention can save us! It can stop a recession and prevent a depression. The free market cannot do that, at least not without massive pain. Before the Great Depression of the 1930s, our industrial economy produced a depression about once every decade. These depressions—often called "panics," like the "Panic of 1837" or the "Panic of 1873"—came so regularly that some thought they were caused by sunspots or some other natural phenomenon. Prior to the 1930s, our 1890s depression was the worst of the lot. It started with the "Panic of 1893," and free market forces needed about four years to sort it out. Since the even deeper and longer depression of the 1930s, we have simply not had another depression! That 70-year record provides pretty amazing proof about the successful role of government, because an activist government is the one main variable absent before the 1930s and present ever since. We used to have lots of depressions. Now we never have depressions.

We do not need to think the lack of another depression is a coincidence and we need not fear that we have simply been lucky since the 1930s. We know what we know about these things. Government has a variety of tools to stimulate and manage the economy and no government since the 1930s has been incompetent enough to let a depression land on our porch. Government can also resolve the milder version of an economic downturn, a recession, though the perfect balance can be tricky to maintain and can be affected by myriad forces. We do know, however, which tactics affect the balance in which way, as I will point out below.

Another certainty we can learn from the Great Depression involves the virtually miraculous power of confidence. It is absolutely true, for example, that when a majority of investors are confident that the stock market will rise, it will rise. Put differently, if more people want to buy stock than sell stock, the price goes up. That is the law of supply and demand, and it makes confidence the essence of a bull market. The same self-fulfilling prophecy applies to the downside. When investors think the stock market will go down, it goes down. That is because their sale of stock pushes the market lower. The stock market boom of the late 1920s was a self-fulfilling prophecy. Some investors were confident and bought stock. As stock prices began to rise, others noticed and tried to grab onto the free money. The more confident the buyers, the faster prices rose. When the first cautious investors began to fear an end to the bull market, they slowed it on their own by their decision to sell. Those not paying attention waited longer, but then they sold too as the market trended lower. Finally, a panic set in, pushing prices lower as almost everyone sold and the market crashed.

The self-fulfilling prophecy that pushes the stock market up and down does the same to the overall economy. Entrepreneurs confident that the economy will grow will hire workers and increase production. You want your workers to be trained and your warehouse full of product when the economy takes off. Otherwise, people will be trying to buy autos or smart phones, you will have nothing to sell, and potential customers will go to your competitor. Conversely, no entrepreneur wants to be caught like automakers have been in the past, with acres of unsold cars and a down economy. You pay to store those cars, you pay interest on the money you borrowed to produce them, and you will have to discount their price if you eventually can sell them. The smart entrepreneur, therefore, keeps a close watch on "leading economic indicators." If the economy looks like it will slow, smart entrepreneurs lay off workers to save costs and gradually reduce the inventory stocked in their warehouses. These are natural and appropriate economic decisions. However, they also become a self-fulfilling prophecy.

When a majority of entrepreneurs lose confidence and lay off workers, it is because they fear that customers will not be buying. But they are making sure customers will not be buying when they take away their workers' paychecks. Consumer spending is 70 percent of our economy and drives it up or down. Entrepreneurs who lay off workers in fear of a recession cause the recession! And entrepreneurs who anticipate a recovery and hire to meet new demand cause the recovery. They do not do so individually, but in the aggregate. They do not do so intentionally, but by accident, as they contribute to the trend within the aggregate. When lacking in confidence, they make rational decisions that kill our economy.

When Franklin Roosevelt entered the White House in 1933, he announced, "We have nothing to fear but fear itself." He was quite right. Lack of confidence crashed the stock market and crashed the economy. Roosevelt's attempt to raise people's optimism level had a

The Left Has Always Been Right

certain effect, but it was far more important that he began inventing various forms of government intervention to reduce our fear of the economic future. The single main feature of his strategy, and the single main feature of government intervention ever since, involves influencing the amount of money in circulation. We can imagine our economy as a wheel on which a gerbil is running, either energetically or slowly. We also can think of it as an old-fashioned waterwheel. The more water that flows onto the wheel, the more quickly and powerfully it will turn. We want a quick and powerful economy. That depends on how much money we pour into it.

When people leave their money in their pocket or put it under a mattress, it takes that money out of the economy and the wheel spins more slowly. Every time money changes from one pocket to another, however, it adds to the flow. The same dollar paid by an entrepreneur to an employee might go to that employee's butcher, to the butcher's landlord, to the landlord's favorite restaurant, to the restaurant's chef, to the person who mows the chef's lawn, and then to the purchase of an iPhone. We can imagine that dollar's path through any pockets we choose and stretch out the trajectory of an always booming economy, unless someone puts that dollar back in a mattress. In my example, that dollar was spent seven times and each time represented another push on the wheel, another boost to the flow of money. During the Great Depression, investors put money in their mattress or their vault and those consumers who had money cut back on any large purchase. Roosevelt responded by pouring government money into the economy, paying workers to build Grand Coulee Dam, for example, or to plant trees, or to paint murals. It did not really matter so long as money went into the pockets of people likely to spend it and keep it flowing. In the case of the CCC and WPA, those workers gained the dignity and wellbeing inherent in a job, they improved the infrastructure of the nation, and they contributed to a growing economy by their consumer spending.

Roosevelt called his expenditure of government money "priming the pump." An old fashioned, hand-operated pump draws water from a well, but only after pouring a bucket of water into the pump to secure a vacuum. Otherwise, the pump draws only air. Once you prime it with that first gallon, however, the pump can produce a steady stream of water, multiplying your first gallon many times over. In terms of money and the economy, once the government starts pouring money in, it entices entrepreneurs to do the same. They recognize that more people have money in their pockets they are willing to spend. Therefore, smart entrepreneurs see it as the time to invest money in new production, rather than leave it under the mattress. When this idea takes hold, the gerbil on the wheel starts running faster and boom times return. The miracle of confidence in the economy does its job.

Some argue that Roosevelt's New Deal did not actually end the Great Depression. That is technically true, since the Great Depression was so severe that it took most of a decade plus a war to bring it to an end. However, the outpouring of government money as the main lever for improvement was clear. That was shown in the first years of the New Deal, when pump priming turned the business cycle around and made a significant impact on unemployment. Roosevelt then decided prematurely to cut back on stimulus spending. A sharp economic drop in the second half of 1937 proved the need for ongoing stimulus, which Roosevelt turned to again in 1938. We can trace the effect of government spending in the economic curve from 1933 through 1938, proving that increased spending stimulated the economy; but it was only the outbreak of World War II which well and truly brought the Great Depression to an end. What was that economic boom based upon, however? Government spending! The economy grew as we prepared for and then entered the war. When government pumps enough money into the economy, the economy takes off.

About the same time Roosevelt was turning around the Great Depression, John Maynard Keynes was developing Keynesian economics. In *The General Theory of Employment, Interest, and Money*, published in 1936, he taught us how to manage the economy and prevent depressions. Many conservatives attack Keynesian economics. We use it, however, because it really is what keeps us from having depressions. Whether we admit it or not, it remains our fundamental tool for managing the economy. Keynes argued that government is the only entity large enough and purposeful enough to intervene and reverse an economic downturn. If the flow of money slows, unemployment increases, and the economy dips downward, he said the government should borrow money and pump it into the economy. That will create jobs and invigorate the flow of money, giving private money the confidence to invest in the economy as well. The government will build up debt, of course, with that policy. Keynesian economics says that during boom times the government can safely pull money out of circulation, paying down the debt. Thus, a rational government should be able to fine tune the economy, minimize dramatic ups and downs, and turn the devastating crises of the business cycle into minor bumps in the road.

There are several potential problems with Keynesian economics. One is that politicians are only too happy to pump money into the economy. (Even Tea Party members of Congress have been caught voting for projects that put money into their own districts. In order to sidestep the obvious hypocrisy, they just refuse to call it "pork" or an "earmark.") But politicians are slow to take away the candy when things are going well. Fiscal policy justifies using tax cuts or increased government spending to pump up the economy. Although Keynes would then reduce these stimuli when the economy is prospering, politicians rarely have that discipline. It is much easier to hand out tax cuts and jobs than to pull them back, but fine tuning the economy in a Keynesian manner requires both. One good example of this problem occurred when George W. Bush was handed a prosperous economy and a budget surplus in 2001. He could not resist offering huge tax cuts, even though that candy was not needed and even though we now see that his tax cuts helped put us in our present dire straits.

A second problem with Keynes involves the potential of inflation, with "runaway inflation" (something we have never actually had!) representing a significant problem. Government fine tuning of the economy includes two categories of tools. "Fiscal stimulus" means that Congress and the White House approve tax cuts and government spending to pump money into the economy. "Monetary stimulus" means that a central bank (in our case the Federal Reserve) lowers interest rates, trying to induce entrepreneurs to borrow cheap money and invest it in jobs. Both approaches essentially involve printing money, which any nation is able to do, and an increased money supply is the root cause of inflation. Imagine an isolated community that suddenly has $200 instead of $100 in circulation. Everything is soon likely to cost twice as much and the money will have lost half its value.

"Runaway inflation" can be catastrophic. Even high inflation, like our flirtation with double-digit inflation in the 1970s, can be a problem. Economists know that a little inflation is okay, however. In fact, our Federal Reserve, which has a primary goal of limiting inflation, aims for a figure of 2 or 3 percent per year. A money supply that shrinks or does not grow at least as much as the population causes deflation. We had deflation in the Great Depression and it was not pretty. There is also a politics to all of this to keep in mind. Inflation can be a very good thing for people in debt. If you pay back a mortgage at 5 percent interest while money is inflating at 6 percent, you are paying back less than you borrowed. That helps you get ahead financially, but that loss of real income is anathema to bankers and others to whom interest is being paid. Inflation is not an absolute evil. It is a variable to be fine tuned, just like the rest of our economy.

A final problem with Keynesian economics involves timing. It is not easy to recognize exactly when an economy needs stimulus. For starters, a recession is officially recognized only six months after the fact, since it is by definition marked by two quarters of economic decline. It is also true that certain forms of fiscal and monetary stimulus take awhile to have their effect. Until recently, our worst problem with Keynesian economics came with the "stagflation" of the 1970s, a period when inflation occurred even while the economy was stagnant and in need of stimulus. That was based at least partly on the severe rise in oil prices after the creation of OPEC in 1973, but it gives an important indication that Keynesian economics is not easy. Without it, however, we would be at the mercy of an economic cycle that wreaks havoc every decade. That is what happened before Franklin Roosevelt and his invention of activist government.

We can now look at our present economy, the worst since Keynes wrote the book on economics, and we can consider the sad fact that members of the Tea Party refuse to read books. Or at least they refuse to read books by a broad range of economists or accept the idea that experts who study these things might know more than they do.

The "Debt Crisis," the economy, the Tea Party, and rightwing ignorance

Our economy started to go bad in 2007. By 2008 it reached its worst crisis since the 1930s, with the threat of an international banking collapse and the possibility of another Great Depression. Then we got mired in the Great Recession, the worst economic performance in our lifetime, and our path out of this crisis has been tortuously slow. In the fall of 2008, George W. Bush and many other Republicans recognized that government intervention was necessary to avoid an absolute collapse. When conservative Republicans in Congress threatened to block a bank bailout, the stock market experienced a one-day crash. That final scare led to a bank bailout that most economists today credit with saving our bacon, even if there are varied opinions on how it might have been organized more effectively.

Obama arrived in the White House in January of 2009 in the midst of the worst economic crisis faced by any president since Franklin Roosevelt. With a Democratic House and Senate, he passed a stimulus bill that took the hardest edges off of the crisis. In this case too, most economists credit the stimulus for bringing us out of the recession. It saved General Motors, for example, when that company and all its jobs likely would have disappeared. The collapse of General Motors would also have hurt all of its suppliers and perhaps even have caused a death spiral for the American auto industry. So the stimulus was a success. But we continued to have high unemployment at 9 percent through 2011 and very weak job creation. There is also a collapsed housing market, with bank repossessions clogging the market and getting in the way of normal sales activity.

Voters in November 2010 punished Obama and the Democrats, apparently for their inability to clean up the biggest economic mess in modern memory in less than two years. The irony of this Democratic defeat is that it handed significant leverage to just those people whose ideology made them blind to the economic needs of a recessionary economy. Republicans have turned the conversation to cutting the deficit, rather than boosting the economy. Their hyper-partisanship also made them ready to see defeating Obama's re-election hopes in 2012 as their highest priority, even at the expense of hurting the nation in the process. Senator Mitch McConnell, Republican Majority Leader, said this explicitly in 2009. Republicans in the Senate have made unprecedented use of the filibuster—the super-majority, 60-vote threshold—to thwart Democratic legislation. Republican control of the House proved even more problematic, with a Tea Party minority wagging the tail of the Republican caucus. That was seen most dramatically during the debt-ceiling crisis in the summer of 2011, with a chaotic midnight showdown that cast doubt on America's ability to govern itself. Standard & Poor's lowered the bond rating of the United States for the first time in history, the stock market plummeted, and the possibility of a double-dip recession increased.

The supposed "debt-ceiling crisis" was a false crisis in oh so many ways. First of all, as mentioned earlier in this chapter, most of the "crisis" involves debt accumulated by our last three Republican presidents—Reagan and the Bushes, father and son—yet it is routinely blamed on Obama. In reality, Obama inherited a $10.627 trillion deficit, about 80% of which came from his three Republican predecessors. Then he was handed a budget already spilling red ink, and the recession made it worse. The debt rose above $14 trillion during Obama's first two years, creating the so-called crisis; but most of that rise was a virtually inevitable result of dire economic circumstances and not due to any policy agenda of Obama. Naturally our debt will rise during recessionary times, because unemployed people do not pay income tax. It also rises because unemployed people get government support in the form of unemployment benefits, food stamps, and Medicaid health benefits. It has risen quickly for three years, because we have faced such a serious recession. That is just what Keynes and any capable economist would have predicted.

Another problem with the "debt-ceiling crisis" is that this phony issue was picked up as a club by a tiny minority in Congress to be used for extortion. All of the debt involved in this crisis is based on budgets and expenditures duly passed by Congress and signed into law. Raising the debt ceiling simply means we pay our bills. Congress has routinely raised the debt ceiling in the past—especially under Reagan, Bush, and Bush, when it was rising so quickly—and at that time no one seriously considered the option of not paying our bills. Tea Party Republicans, however, recognized that this time they could grab the Republican Speaker of the House John Boehner by the throat, along with other halfway rational Republicans in the House, as well as Obama and all of the rest of us. Then they could try to choke us until we gave in to their agenda, supported by maybe a quarter of the American public. It spooked markets worldwide. The lowered bond rating will almost certainly cost our economy a certain amount of growth for years to come. And no Republican running for president in 2012 can risk offending the rightwing base of the party. As a result, every one of them vowed that they would never have accepted the debt-ceiling compromise finally reached that saved us from much more dire circumstances. All eight of them competing in the fall of 2011 claimed they would not have agreed to *any* increased revenues in the face of our debt crisis, even if the deal had been tilted ten-to-one toward budget cuts. This is crazy.

The debt-ceiling crisis is problematic, not just because it caused unnecessary harm to our economy and our national reputation, but also because it pointed us toward exactly the wrong medicine for our present illness. Our debt really is too high and needs eventually to be lowered. That is especially true, since repayment of the debt now consumes such a large portion of our annual budget. But our short-term economic problem is lack of jobs. We should be spending money, using our national ability to create jobs, and priming the pump of the economy. So far the Obama stimulus has made some progress, but it has been significantly undercut by Republican intransigence. It has also been undercut by 500,000 lost jobs in state and local government, by losses in state and local programs, and by the belt-tightening mentality that has dominated our conversation. We can easily get out of our economic trough. The correct choice of programs could also give us tremendous long-range benefits, with investment in infrastructure, investment in green technology, investment in education, and an investment plan to solve the housing crisis. That could turn things around and set us up to compete in the world economy for the next fifty or one hundred years.

Any or all of these investments would pour money into our economy and make the wheel spin vigorously again. Entrepreneurs would recognize the increased buying power of consumers and invest in the economy themselves. By way of contrast, we have remarkably clear proof that the one job-creation measure supported by Republicans—reducing taxes for the rich—simply does not work. Bush handed ever larger tax cuts to rich Americans for two full terms, and job creation remained absolutely anemic: one million jobs in eight years. Bill Clinton created 23 million jobs in eight years and, of course, that occurred before any of the Bush tax cuts were in place. Clinton balanced the budget by the end of his term and Bush gave us the deficits which have put us in this hole. Why would we forget about these enormous disparities in results? What is wrong with this picture?

More tax cuts for the rich in the George Bush mold are hardly likely to help our economy. In fact, American banks and corporations have plenty of money. They have achieved high profits in our halfhearted recovery since 2009 and are sitting on a trillion or more dollars. They are fully able to invest, but they have little or no incentive to invest unless or until they anticipate an upturn in the market, a willingness of consumers to spend. That is the crucial factor in their decision, not the tax rates (and not government regulation). Rightwing pundits and politicians are using our present downturn to try to squeeze out even more benefits for corporations and for the rich. However, tax cuts for the rich are the least likely mechanism to create an upturn or spur investment. Dollars put in the pockets of the rich stay there until the rich see a good reason to spend or invest them. Dollars put in the pockets of the poor, by contrast, will almost certainly be spent. Thus they will prime our pump and make our economy grow.

Republican policies favoring the rich are a problem that goes beyond the present need for job creation. Rich Americans form the one segment of our society that has benefited enormously from our tax-lowering, pro-corporate mania for three decades. That can easily be shown. As mentioned at the start of this chapter, the richest 1% of Americans more than doubled their share of national income between 1979 and 2007, rising from less than 8% to 18%. Everyone below the top 20% has lost ground in terms of their share of after-tax national income. In fact, our policies for 30 years have shifted money from poor people and middle class people to rich people. That includes not only income rates and tax policy, but cutting back on money for education, food stamps, unemployment payments, or Medicaid assistance, as well as the weakening of unions.

This transfer of wealth from the poor to the rich is dangerous and can reach a point of no return. I am not talking about the danger of anger or class warfare. Rather, if poor people cannot buy things, our consumer-driven economy will collapse. That is a good description of where we found ourselves at the end of the 1920s and a major explanation of how the Great Depression occurred. Beginning with the New Deal, we began to shrink the gap in pay levels and the wealth gap between rich and poor, especially through government policies and through the growth of unions. Since 1980 the pendulum has swung steadily in the other direction.

Some rich people see the problem. Warren Buffett, for example, argues that millionaires and multimillionaires have been coddled. They have benefited enormously from their opportunities in the American economy and they should be asked to pay back, he says. Most financial support for the Republican Party, however, comes from those rich Americans who have gotten what they paid for in the past three decades—a set of policies that favors them. The surprise is that Tea Party enthusiasts have found their way so entirely into the Republican Party. They are not likely to be found on corporate boards. Along with Bible Belt Republicans, they are often the very people most hurt by the loss of jobs and the reduced social safety net in today's America. A recent New York Times investigation (2-11-12) describes lower middle class and elderly Americans who rely extensively upon government programs, yet still join in the anti-government, reduced-tax movement. They have allied themselves with the Republican Party of Wall Street, bankers, and the Chamber of

Commerce. They vote for candidates who promise to take away benefits, even as they rely on government benefits. It remains to be seen whether this disparate coalition will remain intact.

"Starving the beast"

One last thread in this complex textile can be seen in Grover Norquist and his version of the anti-tax movement. Almost all Republicans in Congress have signed Norquist's pledge never to vote for a tax increase. That was one reason why Republicans remained so incredibly intransigent in the teeth-pulling of the debt-ceiling negotiation. Their signed pledge destroyed any hope that they might work toward a flexible, intelligent, compromise plan for the problem at hand. House Republicans added another clumsy element to the conversation with their call for a balanced-budget amendment to the Constitution. This too would create a straitjacket, an inability to use intelligence and flexibility to manage the business cycle, as we have done quite successfully for 70 years. An axe and a handsaw are improbable tools for surgery. I defy anyone to prefer those tools to a scalpel or an arthroscope in the hands of their surgeon. Yet our economy is closer in complexity to a human body than to a block of wood.

If we look closely, we can find a hidden agenda behind the anti-tax mania of Grover Norquist and his fellow ideologues. Occasionally they let slip a phrase, "starving the beast." The beast is the government, of course, or a set of government programs that conservatives loathe and have opposed since Franklin Roosevelt and the New Deal. Back in the 1950s and 1960s, the radically rightwing John Birch Society used to talk about doing away with Social Security, which they condemned as socialism. At that time no serious Republicans listened, much less Democrats. After the rightward tilt of the Republican Party took hold, George W. Bush proposed "privatizing" Social Security. He argued that a scheme putting money into private accounts in the stock market would work better. He probably could not have gotten this change approved in any case, but the erratic performance of the stock market in the past decade made it much less attractive to the general public. Social Security has secured an important place in our society and enjoys broad support. Our tax-cut mania, however—which has almost inevitably become a prime reason for the rise in our national debt—could create a crisis so severe that we seem forced to eviscerate Social Security. That would represent a stealth attack, an effort to kill a popular and successful program, not directly, but indirectly, through a manufactured crisis. Exactly the same could be done to Medicare, Medicaid, unemployment benefits, or any of a long list of programs in our social safety net disliked by the right.

The stealth approach of anti-tax advocates always implies that we can eliminate just the "fat," not muscle or bone. Reagan talked about "welfare queens," implying that the poor were dishonestly scheming to get hold of our money. Racism adds a subtle note. Some on the right dislike or even hate minorities and think government money is going primarily to them. Reality disappears from this discussion, the reality of the large numbers of whites benefiting from government programs and the reality that tax cuts might lead to the unnecessary loss of Social Security and Medicare.

Another reality rarely mentioned is the fact that Republican states actually are the biggest beneficiaries, by far, of federal spending in relation to federal taxes paid. In 2005, Mississippi got back $2.02 for every dollar sent to Washington. Alaska got back $1.84, Louisiana got back $1.78, Alabama got back $1.66, and the Dakotas got back $1.68 and $1.53. Reliably Democratic states like Massachusetts, New York, and California got back $0.82, $0.79, and $0.78 respectively. In 2000, thirty states got back more than they paid in federal dollars and Bush won 22 of those states. Nineteen states were net losers, and Gore won 12 of those states. Furthermore, the biggest recipients of federal largesse gave the biggest margins to Bush. Few of those who accept the anti-tax rhetoric of the right want to give up the benefits they receive, as these figures about Republican states and Republican voters sucking up federal dollars seem to confirm. Few voters seem to be aware that federal taxes have gone down for decades and now represent a lower percentage of our GDP than at any time since the 1950s. And virtually no one dares to mention that it might be considered patriotic to invest in the nation in which we claim to believe.

The left has always been right about money, ever since Teddy Roosevelt began protecting us from rapacious capitalism and ever since Franklin Roosevelt taught us the value of government in our overall economy. Some version of the leftist point of view—an intelligently-balanced government activism—gives us our best chance for fairness and equity, as well as for steady prosperity. The anti-tax mania of the right has harmed our economy, lowering our bond rating, lowering our estimation in the eyes of the world, threatening to leave an entire generation at the mercy of high unemployment as well as unpaid national bills, and threatening to kill such important programs as Social Security and Medicare. We can control our national debt. We can deal with the demographics of our boomer generation. We can afford to pay for these things and also invest in a bright future. But we cannot do so with the ideas of the right. We cannot do so with the blind belief that tax cuts are always good, anytime and anyplace. We cannot do so with the blind belief that government is the enemy. We cannot do so in thrall to the Tea Party and Grover Norquist. The right is wrong on these things and their stance is a serious threat to us all.

CHAPTER 5: WAR

It has been my goal in this book to identify those issues on which most of us agree, as well as to argue that those points of agreement come from the left. That is pretty easy on questions of politics, gender, race, and money. When we look at our history, the basic lessons seem clear. A close look at the root issues makes it hard to imagine more than a handful of us arguing for the rightwing alternative. Questions about war might be trickier. For example, Franklin D. Roosevelt, whose presidency I have praised throughout this book, led us through the largest war effort of our history. Detroit quit making cars and started making tanks. We bought war bonds. We marshaled more troops and sent more of them abroad than at any time before or since. Women worked in the war industry in unprecedented numbers, and an entire generation came of age as the "World War II generation." It was rightwing Americans in the late 1930s, people like Charles Lindberg, who questioned Roosevelt for nudging us toward war and voiced their admiration and support for Hitler and Nazi Germany. Yet the right has been a locus of support for war since World War II. This all has to do with questions of when, why, and how we fight. I will try to clarify some issues.

Democracy and war

War is almost always brutal, violent, and costly. In the nineteenth century, as democracy developed in the United States and Europe, some people hit upon the idea that the spread of democracy would do away with war. That idea developed first of all from what is sometimes called the *Pax Britannica*, or the Peace of Britain. During the years from 1815 to 1914, the Royal Navy ruled the waves, Great

Britain became the richest nation in the world, and the British *modus operandi* involved expanding their colonial empire while trying to avoid any wars against nations their own size. Prior to that, Europeans fought like cats and dogs. They had their Hundred Years War in the medieval period, their Thirty Years War in the seventeenth century, their Seven Years War in the eighteenth century, their Napoleonic Wars in the nineteenth century, which lasted nearly 25 years and ended in 1815, and plenty of wars in between. Suddenly, after Napoleon's defeat, no major war ravaged the continent for 99 years.

Europeans had an occasional, brief war during that period, usually ending after several weeks and usually involving only two or three nations. Because this reduction in fighting occurred when democracy was spreading across Europe from west to east, the coincidence of reduced war and increasingly democratic politics led to a belief that there must be a connection. The theory said that earlier wars had been caused by monarchs and aristocrats. Every self-respecting king wanted one or more successful wars to mark his place in history. As for aristocrats, they were the warriors of the Middle Ages, rich enough to own a suit of armor and a warhorse and—in some cases—powerful enough to be warlords in their region. War became the family business. They trained their sons in the arts of war and married their daughters to other warrior aristocrats. These medieval knights in armor also went on crusades or fought national wars at the king's bidding. According to the rules of the feudal system, they answered their lord's call, forming the cavalry while commoners marched and fought on foot. Aristocrats fought wars as a matter of honor, kings fought wars to burnish their reputations, and commoners fought wars only under duress. When common people got the vote, it was thought, they would be too sensible to fight wars for silly reasons. World War I brought that idea to a violent end. Democratic voters on both sides of that conflict committed themselves to this extremely costly, somewhat accidental war as a way to defend their national honor and the alleged interests of their nation.

Many now argue that democracy creates little or no barrier against war. Rather, the convergence of democracy and war created a school for demagogues, those politicians who establish their power by finding an emotional hook that will attract voter support, while obscuring other issues on which voters might disagree. During World War I, governments on all sides nurtured public approval by careful efforts to control the news and spread propaganda. The enemy was made to seem extremely threatening and evil, so that war, though tremendously costly, remained the only possible alternative. George Orwell's novel, *1984*, picked up on this tactic, portraying patriotism coupled with fear of some incredibly dangerous enemy as the means by which absolute mind control can be maintained. Boswell's *Life of Samuel Johnson* gave us an earlier insight into this phenomenon with the famous line, "Patriotism is the last refuge of a scoundrel." It is easy to recognize various types of scoundrel in this context: a war profiteer who makes money while others fight, a flag waver who opts for personal safety while pushing others into war, or even an Adolf Hitler, making use of the German people's patriotism to launch a war that killed at least 50 million people—all of this to satisfy his own megalomania and his hatred of Jews. As we contemplate democracy and war in the American context, we should read the lessons of history carefully and try to avoid the scoundrels if we can.

American ideals and war in the nineteenth century

Most Americans would probably agree on a package of ideals about war, including, first of all, that we fight wars only when necessary and only to defend our nation or our clear national interest. We also probably share the view that we should be the "good guys" in war, fighting only for just causes in a just manner. Both the Revolutionary War and the Civil War probably fit into these assumptions, though some would argue. Other wars in the nineteenth century are a bit more problematic and highlight issues that are still relevant to our left and rightwing views of American war-making. Can we claim to be the "good guys" in our wars? Do our wars fit within our democratic ideas of fairness and equity? The first problem can be seen with the Mexican American War of 1846-48. It was controversial at the time, with Henry David Thoreau willing to go to prison rather than pay taxes to support the war. When Ralph Waldo Emerson visited and asked him why he was in jail, he asked Emerson, "Why are you not?"

The Mexican-American War, which began with a disagreement over the appropriate border separating Texas from Mexico, illustrates the ongoing argument between doing the fair and equitable thing and doing whatever it takes to benefit your own nation. The two governments supposed they had agreed on a border when Texas won its independence; however, Mexico thought it would be the Nueces River and Texans insisted upon the Rio Grande. When Texas later joined the United States, this border issue came along in the baggage. President James Polk adopted an aggressive posture, sending General Zachary Taylor with instructions to march American troops on the contested land, provoking Mexico until Mexico responded. When that occurred he could claim that "American troops were attacked on American soil," even though that was true only in terms of the United States' interpretation of where the contested border lay. Using this rationale, however, Congress supported war in response to the Mexican attack. We then defeated Mexico quite easily.

As an outcome of the Mexican-American War, we not only established the Texas boundary at the Rio Grande, but we acquired the entire American Southwest. In the Treaty of Guadalupé Hidalgo, we established ownership of what eventually became California, Arizona, New Mexico, Utah, Colorado, and Nevada. We agreed to pay Mexico $15 million for these lands, but our entire acquisition of the Southwest was essentially the spoils of war. We had a cover story—that we were merely responding to Mexico's attack. However, it is hard to see that as more than a technical justification, a fig leaf, for the sort of aggression that we later have condemned when perpetrated by Europeans or others. We were clever enough to push Mexico into a war and then strong enough to take some of their best real estate. By the twentieth century that sort of behavior was not acceptable. This war represents one of the first times that our national interest and our alleged "good guy" values came into conflict. Most progressives today would probably be sympathetic to Henry David Thoreau, agreeing that this war violated our professed values.

A second example involves the many Indian Wars of the nineteenth century, wars that now seem morally questionable, if not morally reprehensible. Here again we had a cover story, usually involving

Indian attacks on white settlements combined with Indian savagery in battle. The taking of scalps is one of the most grisly examples of this argument. The gruesomeness of Indians mutilating white bodies after committing massacres against men, women, and children was seen to justify the sort of war undertaken by American troops. One problem, however, involves this question of scalping, which some claim was first taught to Indians by Christian Europeans when they arrived in the New World. Though it is doubtful that Europeans taught Indians a skill unknown to them, we do know that Europeans would sometimes pay one group of Indians to kill off another group. In order to verify payment, they insisted that scalps be provided as evidence for the number of kills to be rewarded. The other problem with scalping as a justification for our wars against Indians involves the many stories of American troops scalping Indians. Taking prizes in this manner seemed to become fairly common during the Indian Wars. American troops not only took scalps, but also women's breasts to be turned into tobacco pouches, and male and female genitals to be kept as souvenirs.

    The Sand Creek Massacre of 1864, one event among many described by Dee Brown in *Bury My Heart at Wounded Knee* (1970), gives a grisly example of white violence. It involved Colorado troops attacking a group of Cheyenne Indians eager to avoid conflict and waving a white flag. Nonetheless, these Cheyenne men, women, and children soon lay dead. The leader of the Colorado militia, Colonel Chivington, justified the killing of children and infants with the argument that "nits make lice." Journalists viewing the battlefield the next day reported that virtually all the adult bodies of Indians, male and female, had been stripped of their sexual parts. Balancing the history of bodily mutilations as well as the number of massacres perpetrated leaves many examples of atrocity on the white man's side of the ledger.

    The other problem with the Indian Wars involves the fact that these wars were very often pursued in violation of solemn treaties signed by the United States, treaties that guaranteed Indians ownership and control of large bodies of land "so long as the grass shall grow and the rivers shall flow." A treaty of 1868 guaranteed Sioux,

Cheyenne, and Arapaho Indians control of the Black Hills, with the promise that no whites would enter the land without Indian permission. After the discovery of gold in the Black Hills, hundreds of white prospectors poured into the region. Instead of enforcing the legal treaties in place, the U.S. government sent a commission in the fall of 1875 with instructions to purchase the Black Hills. Failing in that effort, the government sent troops in 1876 with orders to round up all Indians living or hunting in the Black Hills area, people such as Sitting Bull and Crazy Horse, and place them on reservations. That led to the Battle of the Little Bighorn in June 1876, where George Custer and the 7th Cavalry stumbled upon a large Indian encampment. This was the famous "Custer's Last Stand," a defeat that left 268 members of the 7th Cavalry dead and Custer's group of over 200 men killed to the last man. It certainly was a last stand for Custer and the other 267 dead, but the real last stand was for Indian hopes for victory and for their chance to hold on to desirable land. Improved weapons in the hands of American troops, especially rapid-fire rifles, created an asymmetrical warfare in which thousands of Indians died. By 1890 the remainder had been pushed onto lands considered so barren of resources that white Americans would never be likely to encroach upon them. It is difficult to look closely at the Indian Wars of the nineteenth century and place them into the ethical context I described above: just wars justly fought. The injustice on the American side seems impossible to deny.

The Spanish-American War of 1898-1901, a final example from the nineteenth century, illustrates quite clearly the contradictory relationship we Americans have with war. On the one hand, it is possible to see our war with Spain as an admirable thing, a generous American commitment to freeing the Cuban people from the tyranny of Spanish colonial rule. The "yellow press" at the time was filled with stories of Spanish tyranny and brutality, including the use of fenced concentration camps in which Cuban rebels were held like animals in the harshest of conditions. It suited our anti-colonial credentials after our break from England to play this role in support of a free Cuba. On the other hand, some influential Americans saw our war against Spanish colonialism as a perfect opportunity to develop some colonialism of our own. By the late-nineteenth century all great nations were tempted to prove their greatness by their colonial reach. Furthermore, the American advocate of sea power, Alfred Thayer Mahan, had written about the importance of far-flung naval bases for the fueling and provisioning of any self-respecting navy.

This ethical ambivalence within the Spanish-American War—was it anti-colonial or a colonial grab?—comes into focus when we consider the location of the first shots fired. Although this war was presented to Congress and the public as a war to free Cuba from tyranny, military action first took place half a world away when Admiral Dewey attacked Spanish naval forces in Manila. That attack was hardly necessary in support of Cuba. However, the Philippines represented a Spanish colony in a particularly useful location for advocates of sea power as well as advocates of trade with Asia.

The ethical complications increase when we add Emilio Aguinaldo to the mix. He was leading a Filipino rebellion against Spanish rule, quite like the Cuban rebellion against Spain. Admiral Dewey negotiated with Aguinaldo, gaining the support of his land forces while Dewey attacked from the sea. Aguinaldo later said that Dewey promised him Filipino independence if he would only help with the attack. However, the American appetite for such a strategically located property was too great for our anti-colonial rhetoric to stand in the way. The defeat of Spain led to President McKinley's announcement that we would hold onto the Philippines in order to "civilize and Christianize them." The first oddity in that announcement was that most Filipinos had been Christian for several centuries, converted by the Spanish. The second problem was that Aguinaldo and his followers were willing to fight for independence if the United States would not grant it to them. That is why this war dragged on for three years. It included some nasty guerrilla fighting that prefigured the Vietnam War; and, as American troops struggled to separate rebels from the rest of the Filipino population, they used torture in interrogation and they set up fenced concentration camps quite like the ones so criticized when used by the Spanish in Cuba. If our goal is just wars justly fought, the Spanish-American War fell short.

Nazis and World War II

World War II created what is now often called the "greatest generation." This generation not only undertook the most massive war effort in our history, they fought it to a clear and successful conclusion. Perhaps most importantly, this war offered us the cleanest rationale for justifying a war that we have ever known. It is hard to imagine any cleaner *casus belli* than Japan's attack upon Pearl Harbor, followed by Japan's conquest of properties from the coast of Asia to islands halfway across the Pacific. We built up our forces and slowly fought back, island to island, until Emperor Hirohito and the Japanese military were crushed. This also resulted in a remarkably successful postwar situation in which the Japanese learned to play baseball and Japan became one of our closest allies and friends. The harmonious relationship, now in its seventh decade, continues to prosper.

I will focus, however, on the European Theater of World War II. There our *casus belli* was not quite as clean. In fact, when Adolf Hitler and German forces invaded Poland, followed by invasions of Norway, Denmark, the Netherlands, Belgium, and France, it did not represent anything like a direct attack on the United States. Franklin Roosevelt's inclination was to support those nations suffering under the Nazi boot and to assist Great Britain as it stood against Germany all alone. However, in the face of isolationist sentiment in the United States, he had to camouflage his first efforts. Nonetheless, we now see that the crimes and atrocities committed by Hitler and Nazi Germany, including the intentional murder of millions of innocent men, women and children, made them almost an ideal enemy in terms of just war theory. German behavior was really awful. As a result, our part in the defeat of Nazi Germany and the liberation of much of Europe produced the moment when our reputation in the world reached perhaps its highest point in history. We helped save the world from the most criminal regime in modern times, a regime that from the outbreak of war in 1939 until our entry in December 1941 seemed all but unstoppable.

In anticipation of a European war, Congress passed the Neutrality Acts of 1935, 1936, and 1937, specifically to avoid entangling the United States in any future fighting. That is why Roosevelt had

The Left Has Always Been Right

to move cautiously. At the outbreak of war he inaugurated a policy of "cash and carry," in which we sold war materials to Great Britain so long as they could pay cash and carry the goods on their own ships. When they ran short of destroyers, Roosevelt offered them a "ships for bases" trade, by which we gave up 50 destroyers but gained six valuable naval bases in the Caribbean. When the British ran short of cash, Roosevelt pushed a "Lend-Lease" program through Congress, using the analogy of lending your neighbor a garden hose when his house is on fire. The idea that we would lend the British artillery shells or other weapons of war and get them back must have seemed unlikely. However, our material assistance to the British after the fall of France in June 1940, while they stood alone against Germany, certainly added to the seeming miracle of their dogged resistance in the face of the German threat.

Before our actual entry into World War II—a war in which we clearly had already chosen sides—we augmented the shipment of war materials to Britain by using the American navy to escort convoys to the middle of the Atlantic, where they were picked up by the British navy. Because that subjected American vessels to German U-boat attack, our navy was given permission to shoot German submarines on sight. That seems pretty close to war. But we did not enter the war against Germany officially until four days after Pearl Harbor, when Hitler was the one to declare war on us. Then we made the war in Europe our priority. We helped defeat Germany in several ways: by a massive bombing campaign, by an attack on German forces in North Africa, by an invasion of Germany's ally, Italy, and by the invasion of Normandy in June 1944, followed by a sweep to Berlin.

We did not defeat Germany by ourselves. British forces played a large role and Canada made a significant contribution. Various national groups under German occupation fled to England and joined up with the Allies or stayed at home and worked in the resistance. Most importantly, Hitler's decision to invade the Soviet Union in June 1941 led to the vitally important role of the Red Army in Germany's defeat. The Eastern Front is where the harshest fighting took place, continuing from 1941 through 1945. That is also where the highest level of casualties occurred. It is estimated that at least 26 million Russians died in World War II, split between civilian and military deaths. This can be compared to the 400,000 Americans who died in the combined efforts against Germany and Japan. Approximately 85% of German forces were deployed against the Soviets while American and British troops landed at Normandy and pushed toward Berlin. Nonetheless, the United States played a large role in the defeat of Germany and received a great deal of credit in world opinion.

America's postwar role was also significant. We sent Care packages to Europe, both to Germans and to our hard-pressed allies. Some Europeans to this day remember with gratitude that personal form of assistance. We developed the Marshall Plan that contributed quite significantly to the material rebuilding of Europe and to the "economic miracle" that occurred in several countries. We participated in the Nuremberg Trials, creating a broad base of evidence by which the criminality of the Nazi regime could be established for posterity. We led in the creation of the United Nations and in the UN Declaration of Rights and the UN Genocide Convention, two documents that guide the better impulses of international relations to this day. When Western Europe seemed at risk of Soviet aggression, we created the North Atlantic Treaty Organization. NATO is a part of the grand experiment that has turned Europe into one of the greatest success stories in the modern world: a place where borders are now open and future conflict between longtime enemies such as Germany, France and England seems almost beyond imagination. America was present at the creation of these remarkable achievements. Furthermore, our benign and beneficial role was appreciated by large numbers of people throughout the world. The twentieth century became the American century, not just due to our military and economic weight, but because we were admired and appreciated as well.

Commies and the Cold War

Few readers will have read the previous pages without remembering that a few things also went wrong during and after World War II. Some of our war tactics have been criticized, especially in terms of our bombing targets and strategy. Also, for all the military benefits that derived from our alliance with the Soviet Union, we cannot deny that our ally, Joseph Stalin, was a pretty significant monster in his own right. In terms of the casual killing of innocent people, Hitler and Stalin can be mentioned in the same breath. Furthermore, our postwar relationship with Stalin fell apart so quickly that the Cold War which ensued created a dangerously bipolar world for the next forty years. Several dramatically negative features of postwar American life can be traced to the Cold War. One was the ever-present awareness that a nuclear exchange could occur at any moment and that it might kill us all. Another was the abuse of American values that occurred in the context of the "red scare," especially during the McCarthyism of the early 1950s. Finally, the Cold War did include two significant "hot" wars—in Korea and Vietnam—with high levels of carnage and ambivalent outcomes.

The Cold War had roots that went deeper than 1945. We never liked the Soviet Union and they never trusted us. Shortly after the Russian Revolution of 1917, we joined England and France in sending troops to Vladivostok on the outside chance they might assist White Russians in overthrowing the Reds. Those troops left without playing any role in trying to defeat the Bolsheviks, but the gesture had been noted. During the 1930s, Germany under Hitler increasingly threatened a "push to the East" in search of *Lebensraum*, mixing in lots of anti-Bolshevik, anti-Soviet rhetoric. Stalin looked to Britain, France, or the United States for some evidence of support. None of these Western nations was willing to ally with Communists, however, so in August 1939 Stalin signed a pragmatic deal with Germany instead.

The Nazi-Soviet Pact meant that Hitler gained safety against a potential Russian attack on German troops as they invaded Poland. Stalin gained the chance to grab a portion of Poland himself, along with the promise that Germany would not attack Russia. When Hitler broke that promise and attacked the Soviet Union in June 1941, Russia became inevitably, by force of circumstance, an ally of Britain. The Soviets also began to receive Lend-Lease assistance from the United States. Despite suspicion and discomfort on both sides, this alliance stayed in place throughout the war. Churchill, Stalin, and

Roosevelt met and communicated with each other as the "Big Three." Hitler and some of his henchmen hoped they might convince Britain and the United States to switch sides and join in an anti-Communist crusade against the Soviet Union, but their hopes were entirely in vain. We and the Soviets defeated Nazi Germany together.

When that victory occurred in the first days of May, 1945, the "Big Three" had lost Franklin Roosevelt, who died just four weeks before the war ended. Harry Truman took Roosevelt's place in conversations with Churchill and Stalin at Potsdam in June, and he did not like what he saw in Stalin. Points of conflict spiraled rather quickly out of control, confirming Truman's negative assessment, so that our aggressive posture against the Soviet Union during the Cold War is now known as the Truman Doctrine, an effort to control Stalin's reach and stop the spread of Communism.

The first stage of the Cold War was pretty simple, if not pleasant. Stalin wanted to establish in Central Europe a buffer against any future aggression from Germany, a nation that had invaded Russia twice in twenty-five years. In a meeting at Yalta in February 1945, Stalin expressed his belief that the USSR deserved a zone of influence that conformed approximately to the portion of Europe that the Red Army occupied at the end of the war. Churchill and Roosevelt agreed to Stalin's request, so long as these countries would be allowed free elections. Stalin promised elections, but made sure through various forms of intrigue and coercion that East Germany, Poland, Hungary, Romania, Bulgaria, and Czechoslovakia would establish governments friendly to the Soviet Union. That resulted in the Soviet Bloc, separated from Western Europe by what Churchill eventually named an "Iron Curtain." By 1948 Truman led Western European nations into the formation of NATO, a coalition that placed troops, tanks, and then missiles around the perimeter of the Soviet Bloc. This line of defense ran from Norway in the north, through all of Western Europe, and on to Turkey in the southeast.

Before the Cold War had been long in place, "lines of defense" diminished in their significance. That is because of "The Bomb," an atomic weapon we used on Hiroshima and Nagasaki as we brought the war against Japan to a close. By 1946 the Soviet Union exploded

The Left Has Always Been Right

its first atomic bomb, taking away our monopoly of this overwhelmingly powerful new weapon. The Soviets also built a fleet of intercontinental bombers to match our B-52s as a delivery system. Then they put a Sputnik into space in 1957, making it clear that their capabilities in military science could rival ours and leading to Intercontinental Ballistic Missiles (ICBMs) with Multiple Independently-targetable Re-entry Vehicles (MIRVs). The two sides in this nuclear standoff spent nearly four decades in which MAD—Mutually Assured Destruction—became the somewhat appropriate acronym for our bipolar posturing and our strategy of deterrence. During that period every international flashpoint, such as the Cuban Missile Crisis in 1962 or the North Korean capture of an American spy vessel in 1968, raised the possibility that a nuclear exchange could obliterate the Earth. School children taught to hide under their desks during emergency safety drills were probably aware that their desk would provide relatively little safety from a nuclear blast. Fortunately, the Cold War ended in 1989 without either side launching a nuclear attack, but it is hard to know what role a legitimate fear of annihilation played on the psyche of two generations raised in that environment.

Despite success in matching our military weaponry, Russia had no success in expanding its influence further into Europe after 1949. However, in that year Mao Tse-tung's long-term attempt to create a Communist China resulted finally in victory over the Nationalist government of Chiang Kai-shek, which was now banished to Taiwan. Though this victory by Mao had little to do with Stalin's Russia and much to do with the balance of forces and attitudes in China, maps of the world showed a dramatic expansion of the landmass depicted in red. As a result, some Republicans started to say that Truman "lost China," and the idea that Communists were trying to take over the world gained strength. Karl Marx's confident prediction that communism would inevitably replace capitalism as capitalism had replaced feudalism added to Western concern. Both sides tended to view the Cold War as a fight to the finish. Either communism would take over the world, as Americans feared, or we would prevail and roll back the communist threat.

Joseph McCarthy, a Republican senator from Wisconsin, recognized the political benefits in establishing himself as America's greatest protector against the communist threat. His specialty was the threat of an insidious communist takeover, in which spies and agents would weaken us from within. In February 1950 he gave a speech in Wheeling, West Virginia, holding up a handful of papers and announcing that they contained the names of 205 communist spies presently working within the American government. We now know that he had no names and that he never exposed a single Soviet spy or American communist. But this speech drew national attention and McCarthy enjoyed a brief period in the national spotlight, holding hearings in the Senate and interrogating Americans from every walk of life, especially including Hollywood figures, with the question, "Are you now or have you ever been a member of the Communist Party?"

In the "Army Hearings" of 1954, McCarthy hinted darkly that the entire military elite was compromised by communist spies. He even suggested that President Eisenhower, a fellow Republican, was "soft on communism." Only McCarthy could recognize the real threat, the "red under every bed." We now see McCarthy as violating the very ideals he said he was protecting, the American ideals of freedom of speech and freedom of belief. These could not be maintained at the same time as his belief that anyone to his left was more-or-less a communist agent or a communist stooge. McCarthy was censured by the Senate in December 1954. After this public humiliation he turned more and more to alcohol and died of cirrhosis of the liver in 1957. "McCarthyism" is now a negative term, referring to political suspicion and paranoia that employs methods in violation of basic American values and rights. Ironically, one of our major critiques of the Soviet Union was its insistence that everyone had to think the same and automatically accept the government's point of view. In that sense, McCarthy and his supporters became a mirror image of their enemy.

A Hollywood B movie from 1956 depicted one feature of the McCarthy era: its sense of panic in the face of a threatening but mysterious enemy. *The Invasion of the Body Snatchers* is simple science fiction on one level, with pods arriving in a small town and gradually opening up and taking over individuals in that town, body and soul. These individuals looked the same as before. But they were now the enemy, and they were especially dangerous because they were so hard to spot. This mysterious, hidden danger is the very stuff of conspiracy theories, such as the idea that Roosevelt and Truman were actually communist dupes, working against the United States. When these two Democrats could be labeled "soft on communism" as part of a Republican political effort, it meant that national security raised a high profile in national politics. Given the mysterious and hidden nature of the threat, it also meant that all measures taken to defend the United States against communism were justified. "Extremism in the defense of liberty is no vice," said Barry Goldwater when he ran for president in 1964. The peril of this rightwing idea can be seen most clearly, perhaps, in America's venture into Vietnam.

The Vietnam War

We know the Vietnam War as an eight-year conflict that began in 1965 and ended in 1973. We also know it as a divisive war that polarized the American people into bitter advocates and bitter critics of the war. Finally, we know the Vietnam War as the one war in American history that the United States lost. That conclusion leaves a bitter taste in many mouths and even various attempts to argue that we did not really lose the war. However, our goal throughout the war was to preserve an anti-communist, pro-American government in South Vietnam. After the death of 58,000 American troops and a massive expenditure of national funds and national effort, we simply failed to achieve that goal. Two years after we signed a peace agreement in 1973, South Vietnam collapsed like a burst balloon. Furthermore, although Communist North Vietnam then took over the entire country, no other "dominoes" fell, as predicted by our famous domino theory. The belief that winning a long and bloody war in Vietnam would protect against communists taking over Thailand, the Philippines, Japan, and Australia, before communists landed in San Diego, was simply wrong. Vietnam was not the linchpin in a communist takeover of the entire world.

Our first mistake in trying to understand the Vietnam War would be to accept the statement above that it began in 1965. That was simply the year that we first sent ground troops and began a serious escalation. We had been making mistakes in Vietnam for twenty years by then, mistakes that help explain why escalation of the war beginning in 1965 turned out so badly. Twenty years before we went to war against our enemy, Ho Chi Minh, he was our friend and ally against Japan. All of Indochina—Vietnam, Laos, and Cambodia—had been conquered by Japan at the start of World War II, overthrowing the French colonial rule that had been in place for about a century. Ho Chi Minh had already been the leader of a Vietnamese independence movement against the French. Even though the Japanese liked to disguise their takeover of places like Vietnam, telling Asian people how lucky they were to be part of the "Greater East-Asian Co-Prosperity Sphere," those conquered peoples, whether Chinese, Korean, or Vietnamese, saw very little reason to prefer Japanese exploitation to European exploitation. In Vietnam that meant that Ho Chi Minh turned his independence movement against the Japanese, and that made him a natural partner of American special forces in Indochina. The OSS (Office of Strategic Services, precursor to the CIA) worked with Ho, training his guerrilla fighters and giving them weapons. They in turn helped rescue downed American pilots and otherwise assisted our war against Japan.

Ho sent messages to Roosevelt and Truman, requesting support for postwar independence. When World War II came to an end, he read out a Vietnamese version of the American Declaration of Independence and announced the creation of an independent Vietnam. East Asian specialists in the State Department were pleased with this outcome and recommended that we give Ho our support. European experts at the State Department had other ideas. France, a proud and important nation for centuries, had suffered five years of national humiliation during World War II. First they collapsed in the face of German attack, capitulating in only five weeks. Then people in the north of France suffered under German occupation—and/or collaborated—while the Vichy French government in the south served Germany as an ally. If France was to emerge in the postwar world

The Left Has Always Been Right

as a strong nation allied to American interests, they would need our friendship and assistance. One postwar French goal was to reassert their greatness as a nation by restoring their colonial empire. The consequences were great.

We threw our support to the French in 1945, rather than to the Vietnamese independence movement. Assured of our support, the French invited Ho Chi Minh to Paris for one-sided talks. Negotiations broke down and soon violence broke out in Vietnam. By the spring of 1946 the French found themselves fighting against a small group of rebels, the "Vietminh," inspired and directed by Ho Chi Minh. Their eight-year war in Vietnam had begun. The French were certain that ragtag fighters in pajamas, employing primitive weapons such as sharpened bamboo sticks and booby traps, would pose no serious threat to the French military, with its highly trained leadership, its *esprit de corps,* and its modern European weapons.

Gradually the French had to recognize their mistaken overconfidence and their underassessment of the Vietnamese enemy. A pattern emerged. They could control the cities, but not the countryside. They could control the day, but not the night. They could employ massive firepower in comparison to the Vietminh, but they could not identify guerrilla fighters who disappeared into the jungle or melted into the local populace. In short, the French could not protect their soldiers and officials from ambush or assassination. By 1950, the French cobbled together the so-called Bao Dai solution. To cover their unpopular reassertion of colonial rule, they hoped that this heir to the Vietnamese throne, established as the ostensible ruler, would appease Vietnamese nationalists. Bao Dai, however, a playboy who had grown up as a pampered prince in France, could offer little of substance to those Vietnamese eager for genuine independence, free of French strings.

Ho Chi Minh made a statement at an early stage of the Vietnamese war for independence, a statement that remained largely unnoticed by the French as it later was underappreciated by the Americans: "You can kill ten of my men for every one I kill of yours. But even at those odds, you will lose and I will win." This claim might represent the single most important story line in Vietnam from 1945 to 1975. The Vietnamese, inspired by Ho Chi Minh, showed a tenacious willingness to fight to the death against outside forces trying to dictate their future. France escalated its war effort from 1946 to 1950, always to no avail. By that time the United States had fully entered the Cold War. That meant a partnership with France in NATO and a concern about the worldwide spread of communism, especially after Mao's success in China. However, as we lent more and more support to France in their Indochinese war, it made no difference. Ho matched our support to France with support from the Russians and Chinese, and he nurtured the willingness of Vietnamese to fight against outsiders.

The French effort flagged by 1950. However, we urged them to keep up the fight with the promise that we would pay the bill. We did so, expending nearly three billion dollars in military assistance over the next four years. The geography of the war was clear by then, with Ho's Vietminh strongest in the north, near the Chinese border, and French forces strongest in Saigon and the south. Ho's popularity was very high during this period, with the French suffering the stigma of outside colonizers trying to control Vietnam for their own economic and political purposes. Many in France began to question the value of this war. They were frustrated by the years of fighting, the repeated and failed predictions of success, the many lost lives, and the hemorrhaging of French blood with no end in sight. At a culminating battle in 1954, French military defeat and humiliation led to a French political decision to bring the war to an end.

Dienbienphu was the location of this final battle, a remote place near the Laotian border where French forces had set up a fortified site to interdict Vietminh troops and supplies. Ho Chi Minh's best military tactician, General Vo Nguyen Giap, surrounded the French base with a large number of troops willing to make costly assaults in the face of withering French fire. However, he also managed to get artillery pieces and a steady supply of shells to the high ground surrounding the French. A French one-armed artillery commander, Colonel Charles Piroth, arrived at Dienbienphu full of European confidence. He promised that no Vietminh cannon would be able to fire three consecutive shots before being destroyed by his guns. When two of his three firing bases were captured within a two-day period, he used his one remaining hand and his teeth to detonate the hand grenade by which he acknowledged his misplaced confidence.

Vietminh artillery destroyed the French airfield and Vietminh antiaircraft guns made bombing runs dangerous, so that the French could not even fly in reserves or supplies except by erratic and dangerous air drops. Having thought they were impregnable to anything but ambushes, booby traps, and guerrilla tactics, the French now discovered they could not even win a conventional battle. During eight years of war, the Vietminh had grown from small guerrilla bands fighting in the jungle to large military units, capably led and able to fight with conventional weapons supplied by their Russian and Chinese friends. They had not only strengthened their numbers and weaponry, but also their zeal for the cause. The French, having played a bad hand badly, were ready for a change.

While Dienbienphu bled its way to a French defeat, a French politician, Pierre Mendes-France, criticized French efforts in Vietnam and argued in parliament that the war should end. The opportunity for a negotiated settlement emerged in May 1954. In Geneva that month representatives from France, Britain, the Soviet Union, China, and a somewhat reluctant United States met with Bao Dai and with Vietminh negotiators to discuss a ceasefire. Negotiations stalled, however. In mid-June, Mendes-France became Prime Minister on the basis of a promise to end the war. He dramatically claimed that he would negotiate a settlement within four weeks or resign. Mendes-France's main approach when he reached Geneva was to talk secretly with Zhou Enlai of China, a statesman who had his own reasons to find a settlement, especially to avoid a broadening war in Vietnam just after a peace agreement had extracted Chinese forces from the war in Korea. These secret meetings resulted in the outlines of an agreement. It was then massaged by all parties and a ceasefire was agreed, just before Mendes-France's deadline.

The Geneva Agreement was meant to be an interim settlement. It included a ceasefire with a demilitarized border separating two halves of Vietnam, along with a plan for national elections in 1956. In the short term, Ho Chi Minh took control of the north above the

17th parallel, with Hanoi as his capital, and the French remained influential in Saigon in what soon became known as South Vietnam. French influence quickly gave way to American influence, however, in the south. John Foster Dulles, Secretary of State to Eisenhower, had failed in his first goal, which was to buck up the French. Then he had distrusted the Geneva negotiations, even though the United States ended up pledging to support the Geneva Accords. In Dulles's mind, Ho's takeover of North Vietnam represented another advance of monolithic, worldwide communism. At the very least, Ho should be stopped at the 17th parallel so that this alleged puppet of Russia and China could spread communism no further.

The United States made two crucial decisions in light of Dulles's assessment of the peace agreement of 1954. First, looking for a strong leader for South Vietnam, we decided to put our influence, military support, and money behind Ngo Dinh Diem. He was Catholic, which made him popular with some Americans, even though it had the disadvantage of putting him out of step with the 90% of Vietnamese who were Buddhist. He also lacked any sort of political touch with common people. He never could rival the popularity of Ho Chi Minh, but he was efficient at using our support to defeat his rivals in the south and seize power from the ineffective Bao Dai. He confirmed our confidence, winning a South Vietnamese election in 1956 with 92.3% of the vote. American advisors recognized that this figure was unrealistic, the sort of result achieved by dictators in rigged elections. They suggested that Diem should rig the voting at a lower level of success, perhaps something like 60%; but this proved to be one of many instances in which our puppet would not let us pull his strings.

Our second crucial decision was to back Diem in his refusal to accept the Geneva mandate for national elections in 1956. He argued, ironically, that the communists would cheat and thus the election would not be valid. Our CIA recognized, as did Diem, that he stood no chance at all against the popularity of Ho Chi Minh in a nationwide election. We came to the awkward conclusion that in order to save "democracy"—that is, the autocratic but pro-American regime of Diem, with its corruption, its torture chambers, and

The Left Has Always Been Right

its vote-rigging—we would not be able to let the Vietnamese people actually vote on their future. For nine years, from 1954 to 1963, Diem was our hope for a successful, non-communist South Vietnam. We hoped he would be able to resist Ho Chi Minh, North Vietnam, and the newly-named Vietcong—communist rebels in South Vietnam trying to overthrow Diem's regime.

Diem surrounded himself with family members and other Catholic supporters and employed dictatorial tactics. When a group of intellectuals challenged him to liberalize his regime, he had them arrested. His closest supporter, his brother Ngo Dinh Nhu, ran a secret police system that disappeared dissidents and tortured them in tiger cages. These tactics allowed the Vietcong greater success in their recruitment, especially since they could describe Diem as a puppet of an outside, colonial force—the United States. In the summer of 1963, the first Buddhist priests began dousing themselves in gasoline and striking a match, a protest against Diem's heavy-handed restrictions on Buddhist ceremonies. These self-immolations made for a grisly scene on American television and in American newspapers and news magazines. By August 1963, our CIA passed the word to South Vietnamese opponents of Diem that they had our approval to oust him. On November 2 he and his brother were arrested and then assassinated on their way to the airport and supposed exile. These murders preceded the shocking assassination of John F. Kennedy by only three weeks and left Lyndon Johnson with the decision of how to carry out America's failing policy in Vietnam.

Vietnam was soon to become Lyndon Johnson's war. Truman had made crucial decisions in 1945, 1946, and 1950, each time adding more support to the failing French policy and deciding against alternative strategies. Eisenhower had chances in 1954 and 1956 to let the Geneva Accords do their job of bringing peace to Vietnam. However, that would have resulted in a communist victory under Ho Chi Minh, so he and Dulles tried to create an artificial nation instead, hoping that South Vietnam could prove a pro-American, anti-communist bulwark. Kennedy accepted the logic in place and upped the ante, sending 16,000 troops to Vietnam as "advisors." Their job was to prepare Diem's forces, known as ARVN (the Army of the Republic of Vietnam), to fight the enemy, though American troops quickly found themselves engaged against the Vietcong and acting as much more than advisors.

Each step along this path was a part of the Cold War. Though Vietnam had virtually no significance to the United States—it was not like the Philippines, for example, that we had coveted in 1898—its symbolic value as a place to stand up against monolithic communism drew it from the back pages of American attention in the 1940s toward the front pages by the early 1960s. Lyndon Johnson had devoted his life to domestic politics. In many ways he was one of the most successful of American presidents, with his impact on domestic politics and with a host of popular and necessary Great Society programs to his credit. But his first big foreign affairs question placed him in the midst of a badly deteriorating American policy in Vietnam—the assassination of Diem, the collapse of the Diem regime, and a game of musical chairs in which various pretenders tried and failed to assert power in South Vietnam. Johnson famously said he was "tired of this coup shit." A victory by Ho's North Vietnam and their Vietcong allies seemed likely.

Johnson was very afraid of looking "soft on communism," a political liability for Democrats and a supposed weakness held against them by rightwing Republicans ever since the "fall" of China during Truman's presidency. He manipulated a confusing incident in June 1964 to get the "Tonkin Gulf Resolution" past Congress. This was a resolution the White House had already considered. He now used an alleged North Vietnamese gunboat attack on a U.S. spy ship, the Turner Joy, and made the resulting Tonkin Gulf Resolution into the equivalent of a declaration of war. Frustrated at the lack of progress and his lack of options, he undertook a massive bombing campaign, Operation Rolling Thunder. In order to protect the airfields and the air crews raining thunder from the sky, he sent the first ground troops to Danang in March 1965. Over the course of two years he escalated those first troop numbers until 543,000 Americans were deployed in Vietnam, turning this conflict into Lyndon Johnson's war.

Richard Nixon campaigned in 1968 on a "secret plan" to end the war. He had no actual plan to end war but, as an old cold warrior, he merely hoped that he and Henry Kissinger would be clever enough to win it. They presided over slightly more than half of this eight-year conflict, with nearly 40% of America's 58,000 deaths on their ledger. They also conducted the secret bombing of a separate country, Cambodia, with air crews instructed to lie about the location of their bomb drops. They then launched an incursion into Cambodia in the spring of 1970, leading to another burst of anger on campuses, including the National Guard shooting of four students at Kent State University. This also destabilized Cambodia, helping to create the horrors of Cambodian genocide by 1975.

Just before the election of 1972, Kissinger announced the war was about to end; but his secret negotiations did not please our ally, President Thieu of South Vietnam. So we set aside that agreement and delayed the bitter end one last time, while Kissinger ordered the "Christmas Bombing" in December. In January we signed essentially the same agreement, having made no headway with those last heavy bombing attacks. However, this time Nixon and Kissinger called it "peace with honor" and forced Thieu to accept the treaty against his will. Our most realistic hope was to provide a respectable period before the collapse of South Vietnam. In the spring of 1975, at the first sign of a North Vietnamese attack, the South Vietnamese regime did collapse. Americans fled the American Embassy in Saigon, beating back South Vietnamese employees trying to get into the compound for their own safety. Americans departed the embassy with Vietnamese reaching for the runners of their helicopters, one graphic image of that collapse. American troops pushing helicopters off an aircraft carrier is another. It was an inglorious exit in the extreme. If we measure the Vietnam War from 1965 to 1973, the period with American ground troops in place, those eight-years tie it with the American Revolution as the longest war (until then) in American history. It was hardly the most glorious.

Other elements in the Vietnam War are ones most of us know. American troops won almost every battle, but they could not win the war. We kept a body count and killed both Vietcong and NVA (troops of the conventional North Vietnamese Army) at a ratio of at least ten to one, yet many Americans died every week. Frustrated by guerrilla tactics, we dropped napalm and Agent Orange to try to remove the jungle canopy that hid the enemy. We declared certain regions free-fire zones, so that our troops were free to burn hooches, call in artillery strikes or bombing runs, and kill anyone or anything they came across. At My Lai—not in a free-fire zone—frustrated American soldiers murdered 500 villagers. They shot old men, women, and children trying to run or crawl away, despite the lack of enemy fire or enemy troops in the village. Part of troop frustration throughout this war, and perhaps our greatest obstacle to success, was our almost complete inability to know which of those Vietnamese faces were enemy faces. Children might approach GIs while hiding a grenade. Women were as likely to be Vietcong as men. One result of this confusion, plus our indiscriminate use of firepower, was that more than 50% of the Vietnamese victims of American force were women and children.

Our indiscriminate use of force came especially from our air power, as indicated by Johnson's decision to start Operation Rolling Thunder in 1965. We controlled the skies during this war, using B-52s to drop far more tonnage of bombs than all the bombs dropped by both sides during World War II. Ironically, most of those bombs were directed at South Vietnam, since that is where the Vietcong and NVA were to be found. We bombed the Ho Chi Minh Trail, the supply line that brought troops and supplies into South Vietnam in ever-increasing amounts. A major goal was to wipe out this supply line, hidden by jungle, hidden in the darkness of night travel, and hidden in a tunnel network. Our intelligence predicted it would be impossible to destroy more than 85% of the Ho Chi Minh Trail. We also reckoned that 15% of the supplies sent south would be sufficient to supply enemy forces. As it turned out, our complete control of the air and our constant bombing of Vietnam, North as well as South, could not win the war.

Left and right split quite dramatically on this war. Many right-wing hawks claim that we fought the Vietnam War with one hand tied behind our back. In fact, we used a massive amount of force in Vietnam. However, we did fight with certain restrictions for several important reasons. One problem was the risk of expanding the war, even to the point of turning it into World War III. We chose not to push too close to the Chinese border so as not to bring Chinese troops into the fighting, as we had done in Korea. "Never fight a land war in Asia" is a widely-mentioned cliché in the American conversation about war. Although we have now fought four land wars on the periphery of Asia, we have managed to avoid taking on the one billion Chinese on their home territory.

We chose not to bomb Russian or Chinese vessels entering the Port of Haiphong, though Nixon eventually risked mining that port, and we chose not to bomb the Chinese or Russian ports where those supply ships started their journey. We chose not to use nuclear weapons in order to avoid risking nuclear escalation with Russia or China, including the possibility of total annihilation. We also wanted to avoid the international opprobrium of resorting to this ultimate weapon, with its public relations as well as radioactive fallout. Finally, we tied the hand that might have been tempted to kill every Vietnamese person our troops came across. We did designate free-fire zones, where enemy forces seemed particularly thick on the ground; but other zones required our troops to respond only to identifiable menace. We said we were fighting for our South Vietnamese friends, after all. Killing them without restraint would have weakened our cover story.

Our cover story did grow thin, of course. The most important indicator involved the performance of ARVN forces in comparison to the Vietcong and NVA. Our enemy fought effectively, tenaciously, and to the death, which showed how strongly they believed in their cause. ARVN troops, by contrast, fought very poorly. A few of them were not hopeless, but ARVN leaders had a reputation for corruption and ARVN troops had a reputation for unreliability, for widespread desertion, and for fleeing in the face of the enemy. Was this an American war fought for American purposes, or was it really a South Vietnamese war fought with American assistance, as we claimed?

From 1954 until 1973, it is virtually impossible to remove American motives and American behavior from the equation of what was happening in Vietnam. We tried to separate ourselves from the French, arguing that our anti-communist goals were different from the French colonial motivation; but we were still the outsiders, the foreign invaders telling the Vietnamese how to live and what to do. The natural result in Vietnam was that Vietnamese people responded in accord with their own best interests and voted with their feet. Some Vietnamese attached themselves to American dollars and American influence. We transformed Saigon and other parts of South Vietnam, where we built up bases with bowling alleys, movie theaters, and plane loads of beer and ice cream. Some South Vietnamese benefited from our money and influence. They cooperated with and supported our efforts. Vietnamese in general, however, were more likely to be hurt than helped by our presence. We bombed them, napalmed them, and we wreaked havoc upon their landscape and their gene pool with Agent Orange. In one commanding officer's statement made famous at the time, "We had to destroy this town in order to save it." Many would consider that a description of our entire war, not just one battle. We very nearly destroyed Vietnam as we tried to save it.

And save it from what? Since the collapse of South Vietnam in the spring of 1975, Vietnam has not been a particular problem. First of all, it was no puppet of the Chinese. The first thing that happened after our departure was that China and Vietnam fought a small war against each other. The Vietnamese have resented and resisted Chinese interference in their lives for two thousand years, something we might have noticed at the time if we had paid attention. In fact, the idea of "monolithic communism" turned out to be entirely wrongheaded. Not only did China and Vietnam quarrel after we left Southeast Asia, the Russians and Chinese had been at each other's throats since the early 1960s. Our sense that communists were all comrades marching to a single set of orders was simply wrong. Their national goals outweighed their Marxist comradeship every time. For that reason, our entire approach to the Cold War was flawed, especially our belief that we must oppose every Ho Chi Minh in order to withhold ultimate victory from Stalin or Khrushchev or Mao.

The collapse of communism in 1989 gives us another lesson in the reality-based view of the world. Communism collapsed because it could not compete with Western ideas, Western affluence, and the

Western lifestyle. We first saw this with the construction of the Berlin Wall in 1961. It was built because East Germans could not be kept from fleeing to the West except by force. By November 1989, when the Wall fell, that moment had been preceded by several Warsaw Pact nations opening up their societies, trying to let in fresh breezes from the West. They preferred ideas like freedom of speech and cultural items like blue jeans, jazz, and rock and roll to Russian vodka and doctrinaire Marxism. This was the soft power we had available to us. When Gorbachev chose not to make one last Soviet effort at harsh suppression, chose not to roll Soviet tanks into the streets of Prague or Budapest or Berlin, the gig was up. People in Eastern Europe would rather live like us. The Chinese also would rather live like us, making money while making our goods and—very possibly—eating our lunch.

The War on Terror

George W. Bush was exactly the wrong person for 9/11. I am not referring to his first response to the news as he was reading a book to children. I am not criticizing the national unity he engendered in those first days, and especially not his public statement that we had no quarrel with Islam or with Arabs. I admire those things. His mistakes were rooted in the polarization of the 1960s. As a product of the sixties, he did not imbibe John Lennon's leftwing idea of "give peace a chance," but rather the rightwing idea of "let's kick some butt." The conservative attitude toward the Cold War in general and the Vietnam War in particular was that we needed to be tough. We needed to show our resolve and prove that we were not a "pitiful, helpless giant" weakened by soft, leftwing ideas. So Bush put on his swagger. He also said some things that now seem laughable. He said, for example, about Osama bin Laden: "He can run, but he cannot hide." Bin Laden proved very good at hiding, actually. Bush also said, "Bring 'em on," the sort of taunt he may have learned from Western movies, but never from a primer on how to conduct international relations. Bush's worst mistake (until the invasion of Iraq) was immediately to label our response to 9/11 a war, a "war on terror."

Bush could have responded to 9/11 with police work, with investigation, with foreign intelligence, and with an effort to isolate the tiny cadre of individuals responsible for this attack or likely to attack again. He could have taken advantage of the outpouring of sympathy and support that immediately came our way. The French announced, "We are all Americans now." Even Iran spoke up in solidarity with us. Every sovereign government in the world has a vested interest in a certain amount of stability and established procedure. For that reason unpredictable fanatics committed to a violent cause represent a threat to every nation state. But Bush chose not to isolate these unpredictable and criminal fanatics. Rather, he turned to the blunderbuss of war.

Our first step in the war on terror—an attack on Afghanistan—was not entirely a blunderbuss. It enjoyed much international support, because we had a legitimate target in Afghanistan. The Taliban government really had harbored Al Qaeda training camps. Furthermore, Osama bin Laden, who inspired 9/11, was in Afghanistan. If we had stopped at that point, focusing on assistance to the Afghans and the capture of bin Laden, it might have worked. Bush, however, could not resist invading Iraq, which began to look like his real goal in the first place. That was the biggest mistake Bush made in his war on terror. It was based on falsified evidence and mistaken assumptions, such as the claim that Saddam Hussein had weapons of mass destruction. These claims and assumptions would be proved wrong in the most public manner, as the war in Iraq went from a cake walk to a quagmire in the space of a few months. The Bush administration trusted false information from the wrong people against the advice of our own CIA, because it was what the Bush White House wanted to hear.

Declaring a war on terror and invading Iraq resulted from a deep-seated and wrongheaded understanding of foreign policy, America's place in the world, and America's most important strengths. In particular these choices resulted from the rightwing view that in Vietnam we had not been tough enough, that we had fought with one hand tied behind our backs. Bush's toughness and swagger, his landing on an aircraft carrier in full flight gear to announce "Mission Accomplished," was designed to show the world that conservatives were in charge, not hippies from the sixties. This was no weak and uncertain America, but the one remaining superpower.

It so happens that the Bush White House had discussed just that sort of goal, that sort of projection of American power, long before 9/11. Bush himself had relatively little experience when he entered the White House and almost no experience in foreign affairs. But he had absorbed, along with his rightwing advisors, the hard-nosed, Cold War point of view that it was more important to be feared than to be loved, more important to strike a tough posture than to negotiate a peaceful resolution. We can go back to General George Patton and find an early version. He suggested that we should roll right on into the Soviet Union in the summer of 1945, getting rid of Stalin as we had gotten rid of Hitler. That now seems like an incredible misjudgment of the balance of forces, as well as of the American public's appetite for another even more costly war, and one that would require turning on our recent ally.

General Douglas MacArthur was willing to risk all-out war with China during the Korean War. His insubordination led to his firing by Truman. John Foster Dulles talked aggressively about "rolling back communism" and not just holding the line on communist expansion. After we encouraged Hungarians to rise up in 1956, however, Eisenhower was not willing to risk World War III by sending military forces to Budapest. During the Cuban Missile Crisis in 1962, Air Force General Curtis LeMay and other military advisors to Kennedy suggested an air attack, followed by an invasion of Cuba. Kennedy and his brother Bobby decided on a naval quarantine instead. Once again we sidestepped direct war with the Soviet Union and a potential nuclear Armageddon. During the Vietnam conflict, General LeMay argued that we should bomb North Vietnam "back to the stone age," despite the violation of humane values that would entail. He and other tough cold warriors were willing to risk using atomic weapons as needed, whether in Korea against Chinese forces, or to help the French at Dienbienphu, or in response to our own frustrations in Vietnam.

Hardheaded anti-communists always advised us to take the gloves off. We could authorize the assassination of Salvador Allende in Chile if we disagreed with Chilean voters on how they should be led. Torture could be allowed, in violation of our own laws and of the Geneva Conventions, if it would avert communist success. In Vietnam we could drop captured Vietcong out of helicopters until one of them proved willing to talk, if that was the only way to gain military intelligence. There was always a tougher, more violent stance we could choose during the Cold War. Those farthest to the right were the most willing to cross those boundaries, and even to risk World War III, rather than let America appear weak. They were the most willing to violate American values and international law in the hopes that such measures would enhance our safety.

This is the world of ideas that guided Bush and his advisors in their postmortem on the Vietnam War and in their assessment of American foreign policy after the end of the Cold War. Bush had avoided the Vietnam War himself, as had all of his most important advisors: Dick Cheney, Donald Rumsfeld, Karl Rove, Paul Wolfowitz, Richard Perle, and Douglas Feith. That is what led to their rather harsh nickname, "chickenhawks," an epithet applied to many tough-war advocates on the political right who had avoided putting their own bodies at risk. Some in the Bush White House were also known as neo-cons. These are people whose ideas on foreign policy had once been softheaded and on the left, but who now claim to understand the harshness of the real world more accurately. It so happens that Dick Cheney, Donald Rumsfeld, Paul Wolfowitz, Richard Perle, and Douglas Feith had all participated in a post-Cold War assessment of U.S. foreign policy in the aftermath of the first Gulf War. Paul Wolfowitz wrote a "Defense Policy Guidance" paper, advocating that the United States focus on retaining its place as the single superpower, especially by focusing on certain important regions such as the Middle East. They argued that we should take advantage of the collapse of communism and act to secure our position as the one and only superpower.

Interestingly, the plan that Wolfowitz penned in 1992 was rooted in the rightwing, kick-butt belief that leaving Saddam Hussein in power after the Gulf War had been a mistake. If the United States could find an excuse to invade Iraq and remove Saddam, this would allow us to establish our power in the oil-rich Middle East and create a base for the projection of American influence in the region. This study proposed finding an excuse to invade Iraq. That would allow us to overthrow Saddam Hussein, an unpleasant figure, and establish a powerful American presence in this most strategic region.

Thus it was no coincidence when George Bush, in the immediate aftermath of 9/11, approached Richard Clark, his anti-terrorism advisor. He pressed Clark to find the connection between Saddam Hussein and 9/11, even when Clark told him there was no connection. It was no surprise that the Bush White House constantly mentioned Iraq and the War on Terror in one breath. It was no surprise that Bush and Cheney grasped at every rumor or shred of evidence to justify an invasion of Iraq, despite the Saudi background of the perpetrators of 9/11 and the fingerprints of Osama bin Laden, a man with no affinity for Saddam Hussein's version of secular political authority. It was no surprise that they ignored Osama bin Laden in Afghanistan and planned their invasion of Iraq; and it was no surprise that Paul Wolfowitz acted as a cheerleader, declaring that the invasion of Iraq would be a "cake walk."

We now know that Iraq had nothing to do with Al Qaeda, something that was actually very clear at the time. We also know that Iraq had no weapons of mass destruction, no nuclear weapons program, and no poison gas stored in train cars or other facilities. However, Bush could not resist the chance to invade Iraq in March 2003. This invasion occurred against the wishes of most of the rest of the world. It also diverted us from efforts to find Osama bin Laden, when we had closed in on him in Afghanistan. It diverted us from efforts to establish a stable Afghanistan, after we had overthrown the Taliban government, which really had given Al Qaeda significant support. And it cost us a decade in which we might have used our soft power to burnish our reputation and encourage a better, more cooperative, and a safer world. We were led astray by an experiment in rightwing, let's-kick-some-butt foreign policy. It cost us a trillion dollars or more, about 5000 American lives, and tens of thousands of

Americans disabled in body or mind. It also cost innumerable Iraqi lives as well as ten years in which American wisdom and American commitment to the values of fairness and justice fell into disrepute.

Just wars and just means

It is not easy to know how best to extricate ourselves from our entanglements and false steps of the past decade. It is easy, however, to recognize some of the things that went wrong. We were completely wrong in our stated reasons to invade Iraq. We were also wrong at Abu Ghraib. Donald Rumsfeld, nervously facing a day of questioning in Congress, condemned the behavior of a few guards at Abu Ghraib. Presumably he was condemning the taking of photographs of prisoners with bags over their heads, especially photos of sexually degrading and humiliating mistreatment, the sort of photos that had given America's war terrible international press. What Rumsfeld did not admit that day was his own approval of our intentional use of "enhanced" interrogation techniques, in which guards were encouraged to make life as uncomfortable as possible for their prisoners. Our methods ranged from sleep deprivation to waterboarding and certainly included sexual humiliation among other things. Only the most tortuous reading of American law and the Geneva Conventions could interpret our tactics as anything but torture. Yet we practiced these methods at the urging of Rumsfeld, Cheney, and other tough-minded hawks in the Bush White House. Our subsequent national conversation dealt much with efficacy—which is very questionable for interrogation under torture, by the way—and little with law, decency, or doing the right thing.

Oddly enough, in the discussion of American foreign policy, George Bush's position is known as "idealist," in contrast to "realists" such as Henry Kissinger. Kissinger practiced *real Politik*, as modeled by Otto von Bismarck and other European precursors. That position stresses a realistic assessment of national benefit and implementation of means, without letting values get in the way. For example, in Bismarck's day a Protestant nation under "realist" leadership might ally with either a Catholic or a Protestant nation, depending on its own best interests, not its religious preference. George Bush stressed the moral value of spreading democracy as he launched his invasion of Iraq (especially after his other motives fell by the wayside), which makes him an idealist.

The irony of Bush's "idealist" position is that he so willingly violated American ideals in its implementation. It is very hard to describe our invasion of Iraq as a "just war." We had no appropriate cause of war, no realistic claim that the war was for self-defense, but only the controversial and ultimately far-fetched claims about nuclear weapons and poison gas. It also is difficult to claim that we used "just means." Abu Ghraib represents one problem, and it was only the tip of an iceberg in our willingness to use torture—even though we did some acrobatics with common words in our refusal to call it torture. "Extraordinary rendition" represents another example of our indefensible means. We captured individuals off a street corner in some foreign country and then sent them to another foreign country to be tortured for information. In the most extreme versions of our use of torture, we pretended innocence by not doing the torture ourselves.

We also imprisoned people at Guantanamo, in violation of *habeas corpus*—the longstanding and absolute need to show that a crime has been committed—and without giving them access to any other legal protections. We covered this by calling these individuals "enemy combatants." If we called them POWs, we would have to have given them the protection of international law, which we refused to do. If we considered them prisoners, we would have to have granted them protections according to our own legal system. So we cobbled together the concept of "enemy combatants" and added the thin tissue that we were holding them "outside" the United States, so that no law whatsoever could pose a restraint. Gradually, the Supreme Court overturned various portions of these tortured arguments, but we have not yet extricated ourselves from this more than dubious situation.

The position of the left on all these matters is that we should follow the international law that we helped to create. It represents the best protection for our own troops and our best hope for improvement in human behavior. It also is hypocritical in the extreme if we want to impose international standards on others but refuse to accept them for ourselves. The development of civilized law over several millennia should be our model. Civilized law has reduced the arbitrary and unpredictable use of violence by individuals to settle arguments, disagreements, and feuds. We try to control such violence by the fair and equitable use of police forces and the courts. No responsible person in modern times would advocate the alternative. We Americans spearheaded the idea in the twentieth century that the same reliance upon mutually agreed laws can reduce violence and injustice between nations. It is both hypocritical and counterproductive if we are the very nation that chooses to disobey international law because we are strong enough to do so.

The tough swagger of our right wing and the tough swagger of George Bush relied ultimately and undeniably on the outrageous claim that "might makes right." We would never have accepted the right of another nation to do what we did in Iraq—invade a nation without benefit of international authority or a United Nations agreement and no reasonable claim that it was in self-defense. It puts all of this in even clearer perspective if one were to imagine applying the Golden Rule. That must seem pretty radical to the American right: Do unto other nations as we would have them do unto us? I doubt we would countenance an Iraqi invasion to put our government back in order.

Another standard position of the left is that ready resort to war can blind us and lead us astray, while adding little or no benefit to our security and damaging our reputation as the "good guys." Most of us probably agree that Patton's "toughness" would have been wrong in 1945, if it had meant a brutal war with the huge Red Army that had just defeated the bulk of Germany's *Wehrmacht*. MacArthur's toughness in Korea would have been devastating, if it had put us in a battle against millions of Chinese troops on Chinese soil. Risking World War III would not have been worth the use of nuclear weapons in Vietnam in 1954 or 1972, and it would have seriously damaged our claim to the moral high ground. An invasion of Cuba during the missile crisis of 1962 would also have risked World War III, an unnecessary risk given the success of Kennedy's resort to negotiations instead. In fact, our flexible and restrained response to the Cold War worked out quite well. The soft attractions of Western culture challenged

Russia's ability to control the people of Eastern Europe, and the Cold War ended surprisingly, precipitously, and peacefully in 1989.

Given the extraordinary strength of the United States, it is worth noting once again Franklin Roosevelt's statement in another context: "We have nothing to fear but fear itself." The main foreign policy approach of the right during the Cold War was to stir up "fear itself:" the fear of a Red under every bed, the fear of a communist takeover of the world, the fear of political candidates who might be "soft" on communism. Bush's response to 9/11 was also to stir up our fear, with his color-coded levels of danger and his administration's coordinated exaggeration of the dangers of Saddam Hussein. Prior to World War II, we had no Pentagon. Our peacetime military posture took a tiny portion of our national expenditures. Now we spend more on our military strength than the rest of the world combined, and we possess by far the most powerful military capability of any nation in the history of the world. Safety and security is not a bad thing. There is even a chance we can use our military capability in ways that benefit the world, especially if we do so in cooperation with other nations and with some sort of international mandate. But we can also be tempted to use our military capriciously, carelessly, or even immorally.

Money is deeply embedded in these issues. Eisenhower famously warned us against a "military-industrial complex." We now clearly have one, with generals and politicians moving smoothly into high-paying jobs in the defense industry. That is how Dick Cheney made his fortune, for example. The fear factor in our national psyche since the start of the Cold War has meant that politicians rarely risk voting against the Pentagon budget. Despite high levels of fraud and waste—$2,000 hammers, $10,000 toilets, tens of billions of dollars in fraud and waste perpetrated by private contractors in Iraq and Afghanistan—we seldom complain about corruption in military expenditures. Among other things, that is because members of Congress protect military contractors in their own districts. On a macro level, military spending has been a primary driver of our economy since 1945. That is evidence of two things—the Keynesian effect of government spending and the willingness of taxpayers to allow spending driven by "fear itself."

Any rational discussion of war in our country needs to reassess our expenditures, our choices, and the best ways by which we can assure our safety. We could take some portion of our Pentagon budget and provide jobs building roads, bridges, and schools. That would provide the same sort of macroeconomic stimulus to our economy as defense spending and also make us a stronger nation. Better infrastructure would lower costs for private business, as investment in infrastructure has done for two centuries. Better education would make us more competitive in the global economy, in the same way that superior education opportunities in the United States fueled our earlier rise to economic success. Dealing with other nations in the world without the swagger, without the implicit claim that might makes right, without the imposition of heavily-armed American troops in Kevlar vests and night-vision goggles, would allow us to make friends and admirers rather than provoke enmity.

The United States has a remarkable history of inspiring people throughout the world. Despite our faults, we have a heritage of democracy, of fairness, and of justice that is one of our most attractive features. During the Cold War, people in the Soviet Bloc wanted to be like us much more than we wanted to be like them. The same is true for people in China today. That is an extraordinary national strength. There must be intelligent ways to build upon that, without having to stoke our own fears and without having to slap people in the face. The left has always been right on this, and the right has often been very wrong.

FIXING OUR MISTAKES: A CONCLUSION

The premise of this book is that many conservatives misunderstand or are blind to the American past. It seems hard to deny that we as a nation accept and endorse the fruits of progressive change on politics, gender, and race. One would have to be on the radical rightwing fringe to think otherwise. We are proud of the fairness and justice and equal opportunity promised by our system of government. Anyone who would openly advocate a return to our elitist, sexist, and racist past would earn little respect and have no real chance for political success. Yet conservatives by definition must argue that the conservative approach that was wrong in the past is somehow right for today. On our path to fairness and justice, they argue, we should go this far and no farther.

Similar conclusions can be drawn in terms of money and private property. Only crackpots would deny the government's right to regulate how we dispose of human waste or how we protect ourselves from E coli, Ponzi schemes, or insider trading. But today's conservatives rail against "government regulation." They begrudge the work of the EPA and the SEC and are skeptics on global warming. In all cases they are repeating arguments that conservatives have used for a century or more, complaining about efforts to control sewage and provide clean water or about the "heavy hand" of the FDA and the Federal Reserve. A modern, urban world simply cannot do without some regulation for the protection of us all. We can argue about how much and on which products or services. However, we can hardly deny that government regulation and control has dramatically increased in our increasingly complex world, and that large portions of this regulation and control are both necessary and now accepted by all.

Questions of war retain sharper edges. Some conservatives still think we should shoot first and ask questions later, but that very cliché is almost certainly a definition of unacceptable and unwise behavior. Toughness without intelligence has not been our friend. A sober look at our quagmire in Vietnam produces in most observers a sense that we often got it wrong and took false steps. Communism was not monolithic, but we acted as if it was. South Vietnam was not a creation of the Vietnamese for their own purposes, but a creation of ours in our fear of monolithic communism. As for Iraq, even the strongest defender of George Bush cannot produce weapons of mass destruction where there were none or deny the reality that the Bush administration seriously misunderstood the potential response of Iraqis to our invasion.

This final chapter is an attempt to draw conclusions from a realistic look at history. It will highlight mistakes we can now rectify, if we look to the watchword that the left has always been right.

Job creation by Republicans?

The Republican plan for job creation is always to put money in the hands of the rich. They say it quite openly. Every current Republican candidate for president proposes that we solve our "debt crisis" by cutting spending on social programs, whether Social Security, Medicare, Medicaid, or various programs for the poor, but absolutely not by raising taxes on the top 1%. They insist upon this, even though the American public prefers by large margins that we ratchet back the tax breaks Bush handed to the super rich. Republicans in Congress refused to accept a $4 trillion debt-reduction deal offered by Obama in the summer of 2011, because it included a mere 25 cents of tax increase on the rich for every 75-cent reduction in spending. Even conservative pundits called Republicans crazy for being so rigid as to turn down that deal. The Congressional "super committee" that was supposed to offer a debt reduction plan in November 2011 failed. The members deadlocked because Republicans absolutely refused to consider increasing taxes on the rich. Don't punish the "job creators," they say. Don't give us "job-killing tax hikes."

The astonishing thing about this Republican plan for job creation is that it can so clearly be shown not to work. The supposed job creators have had Bush's tax cuts for ten years. During those ten years, they were better at cutting jobs than creating them. Bush added a mere one million jobs during his eight years in office, by far the poorest record of any president since Herbert Hoover and the onset of the Great Depression. Bill Clinton added 23 million jobs in his eight years. Give tax cuts to the rich, Bush said, just like Republicans say today. Give them the money to create jobs. But rich people do not create jobs for the good of the country. They use their money to their own advantage, not ours. They create jobs in China, India, or Mexico, if they think it will pay better, or they sit on their money if they think it is the wrong time to invest. Putting more money in their pockets gives us absolutely no guarantee that they will create American jobs. For ten years we have tried that tactic and it has failed quite spectacularly.

There is one and only one clear result of tax cuts for the rich—the rich get richer. Our chasm between rich and poor has grown larger ever since Reagan offered us the Republican approach to job creation. The rich also grew richer in the last ten years, as the rest of us have suffered. Republicans are the best friend that bankers, Wall Street, and the top 1% have. The surprise is that so many others take conservative "job creation" rhetoric seriously. The figures about tax cuts and job creation are clear. Any self-respecting journalist should keep this in mind. The next time a Republican offers us tax cuts for the rich and calls it a plan to create jobs—in other words, tomorrow, and the next day, and the day after that—someone should point to the record. How can they keep getting away with such a spurious idea?

The false promise of a free lunch
While insisting on large tax cuts for the rich, Republicans since Reagan have also offered small tax cuts to the middle classes. This has been part of a massive lie, the deception that has gotten us deeper and deeper into trouble ever since. Republicans win support by

promising lower taxes, and they deny that this diet of candy will do us any harm. Reagan offered us the "Laffer Curve," the idea that lower tax rates will produce more revenue. That idea did not work with Ronald Reagan, nor did it work with George W. Bush. Each lowered tax rates. Each lowered tax revenues. And each massively increased our national debt.

Republicans for thirty years have offered us trickle-down economics, the fond hope that money in bulging pockets will spill out into the pockets of the poor. The only measurable result in three full decades is the obvious and predictable one: wealth has trickled up. Rich Americans have increased their incomes and their wealth through preferential treatment. Corporations have also increased their wealth, and the pay they offer CEOs has shot into the stratosphere. Throughout these three decades, a culture of unashamed greed has endorsed these success stories and celebrated them. Since 1980, however, middle-class Americans have struggled to hold their own. And throughout this period, the poor have eaten less and less of the national pie.

Cutting taxes by itself does not represent the massive lie or the free lunch, though it does include the small lie that no one will really be hurt. The massive lie involved the dishonest Republican promise that lower taxes would cost nothing to the majority of us—in particular, that popular programs like Social Security and Medicare that benefit the majority would not be hurt. George W. Bush even added a very expensive and unfunded program of drug purchases to Medicare in 2003, just in time to appeal to AARP voters in the 2004 election and a very good example of his free-lunch politics. The result of lower taxes coupled with no pain on the spending front not only made the rich richer, but also produced the other natural and predictable result: massive increases in our national debt. This dramatic escalation began with Reagan, who tripled the national debt, and continued through George W. Bush, who nearly doubled it.

The only person who intervened to stop the insanity was Bill Clinton. The figures are very clear, though often ignored or forgotten. He increased taxes, balanced the budget, and put us in great shape to face the bulge of a baby boom generation about to reach retirement.

Keep that in mind! Just over a decade ago, in the year 2000, the only concern about our national debt was expressed by Alan Greenspan, who thought it might be harmful in some way to pay it off too soon. George W. Bush simply could not resist the attraction of that bulging surplus, so he offered us the rightwing Kool-Aid of lower taxes. When times were good, his solution was to cut taxes. When times were bad, his solution was to cut taxes. When he took us into war, he sweetened the pot by cutting taxes. He also put wartime spending "off budget," so that the unfunded expenses only showed up in more national debt, not in annual budget figures. Instead of offering us the rigors of discipline and care, Republicans have spent thirty years offering us the free-lunch platform; and it has put us in serious danger. Now, instead of those false promises, we are being told that Social Security and Medicare are on the chopping block, a hidden goal of really conservative Republicans from the beginning.

Turning our backs on the poor
The second great Republican mistake in the last 30 years has been to make us callous toward the poor. Reagan told stories about "welfare queens" in an effort to demonize the poor. Republicans for three decades have argued that the poor get what they deserve, that their poverty is based on poor choices, an unwillingness to work hard and get ahead. While claiming that America is a "post-racial" society, Republicans make broad hints about the unemployed and those using food stamps. They thus add a subliminal narrative of race to their claim that we must cut social programs, adding to their appeal among racist voters. Molly Ivins once described George W. Bush as having been born on third base, but thinking he had hit a triple. Most rich Americans started out at least on second. Most middle class, white Americans started out on first. It is the non-white and the desperately poor who face major league pitching for the first time and need to scratch out a hit in their only at bat. It is not easy. The odds are monumentally against them.

It is not that difficult to make life better for the poor. Lyndon Johnson did it for a few years, lowering the gap between rich and poor America. He did this with only a small increase in the national debt, and even that increase was due to his decision to fight the Vietnam War and pay for "guns and butter" at the same time. Many other nations do a much better job than we do of ameliorating the hazards of being poor. They provide health care. They provide a social safety net. They provide education, including cheap or even free education through the university level. We could do this. It would not only be humane, giving poor Americans a better life and a much better chance to get ahead. This approach would also be cost-effective. It would decrease the expenses of dysfunction in America, from our bulging prisons to the bulging emergency rooms in our hospitals—emergency rooms that provide expensive care to the poor because we do not offer them inexpensive preventive care.

We do not make life better for the poor. Instead, we fall back on the resentments fostered by Reagan and his "welfare queens" argument. We refuse to spend our money so that the poor can have a better chance in life. We argue that it will not work, even though other countries make it work. We pull out the epithet "socialist" to describe any of the measures that intelligent and humane countries use to benefit their nation as a whole. Conservatives also called Franklin Roosevelt a socialist, even though he was saving capitalism, not promoting socialism. We reject the choice of spending more to help the poor by convincing ourselves it is their own fault, they are poor because of the choices they make. But what child chooses to be hungry instead of well fed? What child chooses to go to a bad school instead of a good school? What child chooses to rely on his poor uncle in prison rather than the rich uncle offering to pay his college tuition?

These are not decisions that poor children make, but the grim reality of their lives. Furthermore, statistics on poverty indicate how completely the deck is stacked against poor children. Getting a good education, finding a good job, and making a good income are highly correlated with being born into a middle class family. Getting the best education, going to Harvard, and making a fortune on Wall Street are very highly correlated with being born into a rich family. Even George W. Bush, no one's idea of an over-achieving student, has a B.A. from Yale and an MBA from Harvard.

We are a rich enough nation to narrow the gap between rich and poor, but for thirty years we have chosen policies that increase it. Not long ago we focused our resolve and sent a man to the moon. Now we could focus our resolve and send little children to good schools. We have created an agriculture that can feed the world. We could end hunger in the United States. We could create an infrastructure on which to build a future, prosperous America, as our parents and grandparents did in the 1950s. We could create an education system that would position us for the next economic take-off, as our parents and grandparents did in the 1950s.

We seem paralyzed by our national debt, by our political stalemate, and by the scare talk about the threat to such standard safety nets as Social Security and Medicare. While we worry about ourselves, it is easy to forget that the poorest among us have been the biggest victims of austerity, budget cuts, and hard times. The good news is that all of these problems could be solved with minor adjustments. We could raise our tax revenues back to their level in the 1990s, when we were prosperous. We could lower our Pentagon budget as a percentage of our GDP to the 3% of the 1990s, when we were safe, rather than the 4.5% to which it rose under George Bush. We could tweak Social Security, as we did in the 1980s, rather than privatize it or kill it—a goal of the extreme right since Social Security was created. Above all, we could decide it is patriotic to pay our taxes and work together to make this a better country. We could decide it is patriotic to invest in our future, rather than define patriotism as waving a flag, labeling as "traitors" all those we do not like, and voting to lower our taxes again and again.

The false promise of pushing other nations around

We must also reconsider our relationship with the rest of the world. The United States went a little crazy during the Cold War, as we saw in the paranoia of the McCarthy era. We almost certainly made errors in our response to Vietnam, due to Cold War pressures and fear-driven assessments. The United States also over-reacted to 9/11, at least when we accepted a war against Iraq as a fitting response to the attack on the Twin Towers. Since 1945 we have too often succumbed to fear and failed to appreciate our extraordinary strength and security as a nation. We have not been invaded since a couple of incursions by the English during the War of 1812. We are perched in the middle of a peaceful continent, protected by huge oceans on either side. Few nations would not be happy to have our security, rather than their own.

Our secure position goes well beyond our two quiet borders and two large oceans, of course. We are also the strongest military power in the history of the world, without even a close contender. We have the ability to invade other countries, and no country on earth has a similar ability to invade ours. But this very ability to invade other countries includes the temptation to do so. Sometimes we are even tempted to invade other countries just as a demonstration that we are willing and able to do so. That is one of the best explanations for our invasion of Iraq, as planned by Rumsfeld, Cheney, Wolfowitz, and others. The rightwing response to Vietnam included the fear that we would be perceived as weak and no longer willing to fight wars to secure our self-interest. Demonstrating our willingness, our ability, and our resolve to invade other countries went into the calculus that these individuals developed as early as 1992 and implemented in our shock-and-awe attack on Baghdad in 2003.

It is important to remember in this context the *illusion* of overwhelming force. The French thought that the military skills and equipment they brought to their war in Vietnam would overwhelm their enemy. Guerrilla tactics and tenacity by the Vietminh proved them wrong. During our experience in Vietnam, we possessed the ability to kill every Vietnamese person. Fortunately, we also understood that would be a bad idea. The result, however, was that our overwhelming firepower was largely negated by our inability to know who should be killed. Furthermore, our very presence in Vietnam, killing some of the Vietnamese and burning their hooches, drove other Vietnamese into the arms of Ho Chi Minh and the Vietcong. One big problem in using force is that it inflicts pain and creates enemies.

Another problem in using force is that it tempts us to violate our own values. Every war includes atrocities—rape, theft, torture, mutilation, and the killing of innocents. During the war in Iraq, however, a war conforming to the conservative, tough-guy, post-Vietnam-syndrome ideas in the Bush administration, we embarrassed ourselves with a series of behaviors that were not just random events but came from the top. That included interrogation under torture, illegal arrest, and a questionable *casus belli*—in other words, a series of violations of American law and the international rules of war we promoted and signed in Geneva. Similar issues arose throughout the Cold War. We were always tempted to use the kind of tactics that we deplored in the Soviets, on the assumption that assassinations and "black operations" and dirty tricks were necessary to prevail in our cause. Because our ultimate goals were noble, less noble means were justified. In a minor way, at our worst, we became a mirror image of the Soviet Union.

At our best, we did not mirror the Soviet Union. American history includes many examples of idealism as well as examples of success. That we have lived a charmed life as a nation is closely related to our material resources, but also to our ideas. These ideas have produced widespread admiration and earned us many friends throughout the world. That is a major strength for us as a nation, and it is a strength that has come from the left. Our most attractive features have always been our emphasis on fairness, justice, and equal treatment. Even though we moved slowly toward implementation of these values, we have led the world. It is on these issues that the left has always been right.

৵৵

On all five issues treated in this book—democracy, gender, race, money, and war—we as a nation can legitimately argue that we have something to offer. We can claim to have led and inspired the world. However, little or none of that inspiration has come from the right. In fact, some of our rightwing attitudes toward war have produced consternation rather than admiration, even among our best friends. Rightwing ideas also endanger our economy, and they threaten to turn back the clock on our widely-admired advances in democracy and in gender and racial equality. Reality-based history can guide us. An intelligent reliance on the ideals of the progressive left remains our best hope for a better future. In today's America and with today's right wing, intelligent voters aware of our history should remember this in the voting booth. Our future depends on it.

EPILOGUE: SAME-SEX MARRIAGE

On May 9, 2012, Barack Obama announced his support for same-sex marriage, the first president to take such a stance. Mitt Romney, the presumptive Republican nominee for president, immediately confirmed his disapproval of same-sex marriage. In fact, Romney endorses a constitutional amendment limiting the institution of marriage to one man and one woman. This issue may or may not prove a significant factor in the 2012 presidential election. However, it provides a very good measure of the claim made in this book, that the left has always been right.

Most observers seem to know where we are headed. It is nearly certain that same-sex marriage will soon be a legal and accepted fact of American life, whether that occurs within a couple of years or a couple of decades. Steps in that direction have multiplied in recent years, so that the trajectory seems clear. In the military, change began in the 1990s when President Bill Clinton established a "don't ask don't tell" policy. Less than two decades after the implementation of that important but awkward compromise, President Obama ended "don't ask don't tell." Now gays and lesbians serve in the military without restriction or discrimination, a change that has been widely accepted within a very short space of time. Less than a year after Obama's change in policy, for example, gay and lesbian student organizations began appearing at our military academies and are now taken for granted.

Civil unions became the next step forward. Vermont in 2000 was the first state to legalize such arrangements for same-sex couples.

Then, in 2003, the Massachusetts Supreme Court declared same-sex marriage legal. Massachusetts now is at the center of a small group of northeastern states—along with New York, Connecticut, New Hampshire, and Vermont—that have legalized same-sex marriage. Same-sex marriage in Iowa came by way of the State Supreme Court, in Washington by the state legislature (subject to a possible public vote), and in California by the Ninth Circuit Court, if its decision stands. The U.S. Supreme Court may soon approve, expand, or reject that California ruling.

This seismic shift within less than a decade has occurred in the face of significant rightwing anger and opposition. Thirty-two states have written into their constitutions the insistence that legal marriage can only occur between one man and one woman. It is worth noting that a very similar number of American states banned marriage between blacks and whites as recently as fifty years ago. Soon the banning of same-sex marriage is almost certainly going to look as inappropriate and out of date as those anti-miscegenation laws. Polls show that a majority of Americans now accept same-sex marriage. More importantly, very few Americans under the age of forty see gay marriage as controversial. When those now over forty die off, or when they are seriously outnumbered, their opposition to same-sex marriage will likely die with them.

This is not just a question of demographics and changing social values. It is also deeply rooted in two principles vital to American democracy. One is the insistence on equality of treatment before the law. Surely, the same principle that bars discrimination based upon gender and race requires that gays and lesbians should similarly enjoy full and equal protection under law. Americans long saw an unbridgeable gap between men and women as well as between whites and blacks. It did not seem necessary or appropriate to grant women or blacks equal rights. Due to our progressive heritage, we now see how wrong that was. Many conservative Americans today see an unbridgeable gap between heterosexuals and homosexuals. Both groups are human beings, however. So long as same-sex couples cannot marry, homosexuals are denied the full range of legal rights attached to marriage and available to heterosexuals. That likely will soon be acknowledged as a clear violation of equality before the law.

The second vital principle involves our separation of church and state. Most opposition to same-sex marriage quickly reveals its religious roots, whether in sermons, in letters to the editor, or in statements on the floor of Congress. God intended marriage for one man and one woman, we are told. The Bible condemns homosexuality, we are told. Acknowledgement of same-sex marriage would be an endorsement of moral degradation, we are told, the legal approval of behavior that is an abomination in God's sight. These are religious beliefs, without foundation in secular legal principle. In fact, it is difficult to find hard-edged secular opponents of same-sex marriage, opponents who do not call upon their version of God as the foundation for their point of view. Opposition springs almost entirely from that segment of the Christian community that considers same-sex relationships a sin. There is a simple answer for their concern, of course. They can choose to have heterosexual relationships. They can stay true to their beliefs. But they should have no right to force their beliefs on the rest of the nation.

The best democracy is tolerant. The best democracy is pluralist. The best democracy grants equal rights to all. We know that this nation has always included Catholics as well as Protestants—often in bitter opposition to each other—plus Deists, Jews, Muslims, Buddhists, pagans, atheists, and other believers of every description. The separation of church and state has meant that each of these belief systems is tolerated, at least in principle. We now have improved considerably in our recognition that they should be tolerated in reality as well. The best of American democracy has been our willingness gradually to acknowledge that "all men" and "all women" really are "created equal." Differences in gender, race, or religion should not mean differences in legal rights, nor should differences in sexual orientation. The left is right on this. Even conservatives will accept that before too long.

Made in the USA
Charleston, SC
15 October 2012